THE ECONOMY AND SUICIDE
ECONOMIC PERSPECTIVES ON SUICIDE

THE ECONOMY AND SUICIDE
ECONOMIC PERSPECTIVES ON SUICIDE

BY

DAVID LESTER AND BIJOU YANG

CENTER FOR THE STUDY OF SUICIDE   DEPARTMENT OF ECONOMICS
BLACKWOOD, NEW JERSEY   DREXEL UNIVERSITY

Art Director: Maria Ester Hawrys
Assistant Director: Elenor Kallberg
Graphics: Susan A. Boriotti, and Frank Grucci
Manuscript Coordinator: Phyllis Gaynor
Book Production: Gavin Aghamore, Joanne Bennette, Michelle Keller
Christine Mathosian and Tammy Sauter
Circulation: Iyatunde Abdullah, Cathy DeGregory and Annette Hellinger

Library of Congress Cataloging-in-Publication Data
available upon request

ISBN 1-56072-423-4

Copyright © 1997 by Nova Science Publishers, Inc.
6080 Jericho Turnpike, Suite 207
Commack, New York 11725
Tele. 516-499-3103 Fax 516-499-3146
E Mail Novascil@aol.com

Printed in the United States of America

CONTENTS

PART 1: INTRODUCTION

PART 2: THEORIES OF SUICIDE AND THE ECONOMY

PART 5: CONCLUSIONS

PART ONE:

INTRODUCTION

CHAPTER 1

INTRODUCTION

It is a common belief that the Great Depression in the 1920s led to an increase in the suicide rate among Americans, especially those affected by the stock market crash. The media helped along this belief with stories that bankers and business leaders jumped out of windows in Manhattan to their death on the streets below.

There is some truth in this, but there are also misconceptions. While the suicide rate in the United States did increase from 1925 to 1932, part of the reason for this was that the number of states reporting deaths to the United States government increased during this period, with the more western states -- which have above average suicide rates -- beginning to report for the first time.

However, John Kenneth Galbraith (1954) has noted that, although the number of suicides also rose in New York City during the period of 1925 to 1932, in 1929, the year of the Great Crash, there were only 1,331 United States suicides in "black" October compared to 1,344 in the following November, and no more than in the January, February or September of 1929.

Thus, perhaps the Great Depression did lead to increased suicidal behavior in Americans, but the suicide rates appear to have responded more to the gradual changes in the economic conditions rather than immediately to specific events.

While the phenomenon of large numbers of stockbrokers and bankers jumping to their death on Wall Street during the Great Depression may, therefore, be a myth, there is good evidence that the economy may have an impact on suicidal behavior, particular for certain age groups. Our aim in this book is to explore this evidence by examining existing sociological theories of suicide which have discussed the impact of economic conditions, by applying economic theories of choice to suicidal behavior, and by reviewing published research on the association between the economy and suicide.

Some scholars believe that suicidal behavior results in a cost to the society. Before reviewing theories and research on the relationship between the economy and suicidal behavior, efforts to estimate the economic cost of suicidal behavior to the society are reviewed in Chapter 2.

Part Two of this book describes the sociological theories which have tried to explain the relationship between economic conditions and suicidal behavior. Chapters 3, 4 and 5 present three theories of this relationship proposed, respectively, by Emile Durkheim, by Ralph Ginsberg, and by Andrew Henry and James Short. In Chapter 6 these theories are rephrased in mathematical terms and their predictions for the relationship between the business cycle and the suicide rate are derived logically. Some empirical tests of these predictions are also presented in Chapter 6.

Part Three presents four theories of suicide which are based on microeconomic foundations. In Chapter 7, a cost-benefit analysis and a demand and supply framework proposed by the present authors are applied to suicidal behavior. An early econometric analysis of suicide by Hamermesh and Soss is presented in Chapter 8. McCain applies his cognitive model of human functioning, which involves impulse-filtering, to suicide in Chapter 9, while Huang applies a labor force participation model to suicide in Chapter 10 by viewing the choice of life versus death as entering or leaving the "life market." Chapter 11 presents a review of other economic models of suicide.

Part Four reviews the empirical research on the relationship between economic conditions and suicidal behavior. Among the relevant economic factors, the most thoroughly investigated is the role of unemployment. Chapter 12 reviews this research from cross-sectional and longitudinal perspectives and for societies and individuals. Research on other economic variables, such as industrialization and income inequality, are reviewed in Chapter 13. The association between the quality of life, aspects of which involve economic variables, and suicide is explored in Chapter 14. Finally, our own research on the relative role played by economic and social variables in determining the suicide rate is presented in Chapter 15.

Finally, Chapter 16 in Part Five summarizes the conclusions that can be drawn from this review.

REFERENCE

Galbraith, J. K. *The Great Crash, 1929.* Boston: Houghton-Mifflin, 1954.

CHAPTER 2

THE ECONOMIC COSTS OF SUICIDE

E pidemiological studies suggest that major depressive illness affects about two percent of the population of the United States, and there are about 30,000 suicides each year. What economic cost do these behaviors involve for the nation? Stoudemire, et al. (1986) made an effort to estimate this cost.

For those suffering from a major depressive illness, there are both direct costs and indirect costs. The direct costs include the cost of treatment (such as physician visits, hospitalization, pharmaceuticals and travel costs when seeking care), while the indirect costs accrue from the loss of productivity of those who have a major depression. For those who commit suicide, the costs are mainly indirect.

DEPRESSIVE ILLNESS

Using data from studies conducted under the auspices of the National Institute of Mental Health, Stoudemire estimated that the number of cases of major depressive illness in a six month period in 1980 was 4.8 million. From other epidemiological studies, Stoudemire estimated that affective disorders accounted for about half a million hospital admissions in 1980, 7.4 million hospital days, and 13.3 million physician visits.

For inpatient care, the total cost came to 1.3 billion dollars. For outpatient care, the cost was 0.6 billion dollars. Other costs (including medication) came to 0.2 billion dollars, giving a grand total of 2.1 billion dollars.

The indirect costs of major depressive illnesses were based on an estimate of 5.7 million treated cases and 2.8 million untreated cases in 1980. Stoudemire estimated that these cases led to 127 million days lost involving treatment and 92 million days lost over and above the treatment days. Using data on the proportion of men and women in the labor force, Stoudemire estimated a loss of 10.0 billion dollars in earnings.

Many persons with depressive illness commit suicide. Stoudemire estimated that about 60 percent of all suicides have a major depressive illness. In 1980, there were 26,869 suicides, and Stoudemire estimated that the suicides of those with major depressive illness (using sex-specific estimates of discounted lifetime earnings) involved an indirect cost of 4.2 billion dollars.

Thus the total cost of major depressive illness in 1980 was estimated to be 2.1 billion dollars for direct costs, 10.0 billion dollars due to lost productivity, and 4.2 billion dollars due to mortality from suicide. These costs add up to 16.3 billion dollars.

It should be noted that the suicides of those with major depressive disorders eliminates the need for treatment for these individuals in future years and so results in savings in direct costs. Thus, the direct costs for treatment might have been higher, for example, in 1980, if some of those suffering from a major depressive illness in earlier years had not committed suicide.

More recent estimates of the cost to the society for depressive disorders are four times the amount estimated by Stoudemire (Miller, 1993).

SUICIDE

Stoudemire's estimate for the indirect cost as a result of the suicide of those with a major depressive illness was 4.2 billion dollars. This was based on an estimate of 60 percent of suicides having a major depressive illness. From this, we can estimate that the indirect costs of all of the suicides through lost lifetime earnings would be 7 billion dollars.

In addition, suicides also involve medical and legal costs in the efforts to revive suicides and to certify the deaths, but these costs are probably dwarfed by the indirect costs. For example, Weinstein and Saturno (1989) estimated the economic effects of a single youth suicide (among those aged 15 to 24 years of age) as $431,000 from lost life-time earnings (roughly $10,400 per year) and $1,067 in medicolegal expenses.

In addition to the behavior of suicide in which the person dies, there are many attempts at suicide each year where the individual survives. It is difficult to count the number of attempts at suicide each year because many attempters do not require medical attention and so do not come to the attention of the authorities. However, it has been estimated by Farberow and Shneidman (1961) that there at least eight suicide attempts for every completed suicide (the technical term for those who die). Thus, if there are 30,000 completed suicides in one year, there may be upwards of 240,000 attempted suicides.

Many attempted suicides require medical care, and a good proportion of them receive psychological and psychiatric treatment. These attempters will be lost to the labor force during this period, incurring additional economic costs. For example, Rodger and Scott (1995) estimated that the medical costs of treating an attempted suicide for merely subsequent suicidal behavior was thirty-four thousand British Pounds in 1986-1987 prices.

CONCLUSIONS

It can be seen that the economic costs of suicide may be considerable, and in addition there is the psychological pain and suffering of both the people who commit suicide and those who survive the suicide of a loved one. Understanding and preventing suicidal behavior is clearly an important economic task for our society.

However, Lester (1995) has suggested that these estimates may be gross exaggerations of the true cost of suicide. Applying the work of Viscuso (1994) on the economic impact of diseases caused by smoking, Lester noted that (a) suicides avoid the cost of treating the underlying psychiatric disorder had the person continued living, (b) estimates of the life-time earnings do not take into account the fact that many suicides are marginal people who do not function productively in the workplace, and (c) premature death reduces the eventual costs of later medical treatments, nursing home care, and pension and social security payments. Viscuso concluded that each package of cigarettes sold saves the society some money, and the same might be true of suicides. We must beware of selectively choosing economic data to fit our perspective.

REFERENCES

Farberow, N. L., & Shneidman, E. S. *The cry for help*. New York: McGraw-Hill, 1961.

Lester, D. Estimating the true economic cost of suicide. *Perceptual & Motor Skills*, 1995, 80, 746.

Miller, M. W. Dark days: the staggering cost of depression. *Wall Street Journal*, 1993, December 2, B1, B8.

Rodger, C. R., & Scott, A. I. F. Frequent deliberate self-harm. *Scottish Medical Journal*, 1995, 40, 10-13.

Stoudemire, A., Frank, R., Hedemark, N., Kamlet, M., & Blazer, D. The economic burden of depression. *General Hospital Psychiatry*, 1986, 8, 387-394.

Viscuso, W. K. *Cigarette taxation and the social consequences of smoking*. Cambridge, MA: NBER, 1994.

Weinstein, M. C., & Saturno, P. J. Economic impact of youth suicide and suicide attempts. *Report of the Secretary's Task Force on Youth Suicide*, 1989, 4, 82-93. Washington, DC: United States Government Printing Office.

PART TWO:

THEORIES OF SUICIDE AND THE ECONOMY

CHAPTER 3

DURKHEIM

E mile Durkheim (1897) published a volume on suicide that has proven to be the seminal sociological work on suicide for the twentieth century. In it, he proposed that two characteristics of societies were central for the understanding of suicide: social integration and social regulation.

The degree of *social integration* referred to the extent to which the members of a society shared beliefs and sentiments, interest in one another, and a common sense of devotion to common goals. Later sociologists have stressed more the number, type, and durability of social relationships in a society as critical for the definition of social integration. Suicidal behavior will be frequent in societies where the level of social integration is very low, and the type of suicide in this situation is called *egoistic* suicide. Suicide will also be frequent in societies where the level of social integration is very high, and the type of suicide in this situation is called *altruistic* suicide.

The members of a society are *socially regulated* insofar as the society controls their emotions and motivations. Suicide will be common where social regulation is very low, giving rise to *anomic* suicide, and where social regulation is very high, giving rise to *fatalistic* suicide.

Because of the importance of Durkheim's ideas, there have been many detailed analyses and criticisms of his ideas. Some of these have been explored elsewhere (Lester, 1989). Rather than reviewing these critiques here, we will focus on Durkheim's hypotheses about the effect of the economy on suicide.

THE ECONOMY AND SUICIDE

Durkheim considered the effects of the economy on suicide in his chapter on anomic suicide. He noted first that financial crises led to an immediate rise in the suicide rate, documenting this with examples from Vienna in 1873, Frankfurt-on-Main in 1874, and Paris in 1882. He also noted that, when the number of bankruptcies rose in a society, the suicide rate also increased. (These time series analyses were presented quite simply, with none of the statistical sophistication of modern times.)

Durkheim doubted that these financial crises resulted in higher suicide rates because of the increased poverty they produced. He suggested that suicide rates rose also during *fortunate crises* which enhanced a nation's prosperity. In support of this suggestion, he noted that the increased industrialization in Italy after its unification was accompanied by an increased suicide rate. In Prussia, too, the growth in glory and power as it annexed new provinces was accompanied by an increase in the suicide rate. Suicide rates rose during the World Expositions in 1878 and 1889.

Durkheim moved to a regional (ecological) approach by noting next that poverty in nations was not associated with a high suicide rate. He noted that both Ireland and Calabria (in Spain) had a high rate of poverty but low suicide rates.

Thus, Durkheim concluded that financial crises do not lead to a higher suicide rate because of the increased poverty, but rather because they disturb the *collective order*.

Durkheim suggested that people differ from other animals in that their desires often outstrip the means at their disposal for satisfying them. He felt that people's desires easily become unlimited and, therefore, insatiable. The only check on these desires is from external sources which must provide the moral forces to restrain his desires, and only society can play this moderating role. Society must set a limit on desires and must also estimate the appropriate rewards for its members.

Economic disasters cast some people into lower statuses in which they must restrain their desires still further and accept still fewer rewards. But the speed of such disasters gives the society no time to prepare its members for such abrupt changes. Since the people cannot adjust quickly to the new conditions, their suffering is increased.

Similarly, during periods of prosperity, the conditions of life change without adequate time for the society to prepare the members of the society for this change. The increasing prosperity removes the limits on people's desires without new limits being imposed. There is no restraint upon aspirations.

In both of these types of crisis (disasters and prosperity), the result is a reduction in the strength of social regulation and an accompanying increase in anomie.

Durkheim argued that poverty protects against suicide because it, in itself, is a restraint. Lack of resources and lack of power set automatic limits on people's desires. Wealth, on the other hand, leads to increased power and suggests the possibility of unlimited rewards.

In viewing the growth of industrialization in the nineteenth century, Durkheim saw the rapid expansion of trade and commerce as leading to the removal of perceived restraints on desires. Thus, anomie was increasing along with this industrial development, leading to higher suicide rates. Durkheim felt that this process would be more noticeable in those engaged in the industries and businesses which were expanding most and in the higher social classes. The fever of business penetrates less forcefully to agriculture, he thought, and the lower classes have their horizons limited by the presence of those above them.

The suicide that results from man's activity lacking regulation and the consequent suffering, Durkheim named *anomic suicide.*

DISCUSSION

In Chapter 6, we will present a formal economic model that describes Durkheim's theory of the relationship between the economy and suicide, but suffice it to say here that Durkheim's theory results in a V-shaped function relating the economy and suicide. Suicide is more common during times of both extreme economic contraction and extreme economic expansion and less common in times of moderate economic activity.

REFERENCES

Durkheim, E. *Le suicide*. Paris: Alcan, 1897.

Lester, D. *Suicide from a sociological perspective*. Springfield, IL: Charles Thomas, 1989.

CHAPTER 4

GINSBERG

R alph Ginsberg (1966) reinterpreted Durkheim's notion of anomie in terms of the psychological concept of level of aspiration. One of the examples of anomic suicide given by Durkheim was that the suicide rate increased during financial crashes and during financial booms. Suicide resulting from these financial changes was seen as an example of anomic suicide since the environmental deficit in external restraint that accompanied these changes allowed the desires of the individual to range freely and without control. With no external restraints, the desires become unlimited and insatiable. This is anomie.

Ginsberg noted that anomie arose from the unhappiness or dissatisfaction of individuals. He postulated that anomie was a direct function of the dissatisfaction of the individual, which itself was a direct function of the discrepancy between the actual reward that the individual was receiving and his level of aspiration. In the *normal process*, internalized legitimate norms which are dependent upon the individual's social position regulate changes in the individual's level of aspiration. The level of aspiration remains proportional to the rewards, and the individual is relatively satisfied. In the *anomic process*, the level of aspiration, freed from external constraints, runs away from the rewards, resulting in unhappiness for the individual.

Although psychological evidence points to the fact that the level of a person's aspiration adjusts to the present level of rewards at a rate proportional to the degree of dissatisfaction (March and Simon, 1958), Durkheim's notion was simpler and implied that aspirations adjust to the level of reward directly rather than to dissatisfaction.

Ginsberg formalized Durkheim's implicit propositions as follows: (a) as rewards increase, aspirations tend to increase, and as rewards decrease, aspirations tend to decrease, and (b) the rate of change of aspirations is a function of the extent to which rewards increase or decrease. Ginsberg noted that modern theories of aspiration also assume the converse -- the reward obtained is affected by the level of aspiration of the individual. The level of aspiration affects the behavior of the person, which in turn affects the rewards he obtains.

Ginsberg suggested that, if an individual sees no relationship between what he does and the rewards he obtains, then there is no tendency for aspirations to change. For the level of aspiration to change, the individual must possess and feel a *sense of efficacy*. Although Durkheim paid little attention to this variable, Ginsberg felt that Durkheim implicitly accepted it. As the individual's sense of efficacy increases, his aspirations tend to drop. The sense of efficacy is an intervening variable between changes in his rewards and his level of aspirations.

When rewards increase faster than aspirations, we have a normal process, but when aspirations increase faster than rewards, we have an anomic process. In the anomic process aspirations mount at an increasingly faster rate, running away from rewards, and this is what happens to some individuals during financial booms. Similarly, when rewards decrease and aspirations decrease at a lesser rate, leveling off at some constant value and converging with rewards, we have a normal process. When aspirations decrease at an increasing rate and never reach an equilibrium with rewards, we have an anomic process, and this is what happens to some individuals during financial crashes.

Durkheim held that the difference between the normal and the anomic process was that, in the anomic process, the norms of the society have no control over aspiration change whereas in the normal process they do. In the absence of social control, aspirations change anomically. Social control can be seen either as a set of internalized controls resulting in a modification and toning down of the individual's desires or as a set of external regulatory forces opposed to the individual's desires. As a result of social control, therefore, aspirations change according to this normal process. Societal norms provide an upper and lower limit within which aspirations and rewards remain in the normal process. Ginsberg called this the *interval of distributive justice.*

Ginsberg attempted to deduce the discrepancy between aspirations and rewards at different points of the business cycle and to predict the association between business prosperity and the suicide rate. In formal terms, Ginsberg assumed that (a) the suicide rate in a given society varied directly with the average amount of dissatisfaction in that society, (b) fluctuations in the economy determine the average rewards available, (c) the average dissatisfaction depends upon the average aspirations as well as the average rewards, and (d) economic aspirations are governed by the following five postulates:

(1) When rewards are increasing, the individual will expect them to continue to increase and raise his aspirations accordingly.

(2) As long as the rate of change of rewards is increasing and as long as rewards are cumulative, the individual will expect them to continue to cumulate and raise his aspirations to meet the even higher expected rewards.

(3) When rewards are decreasing, the individual will expect them to continue to decrease and lower his aspirations accordingly.

(4) As long as the rate of fall of rewards is increasing and as long as the drops are cumulative, the individual will expect them to continue to cumulate and lower his aspirations to meet the even lower expected rewards.

(5) When the rate of change in rewards is decreasing, the rate of change of aspiration will decrease even faster in anticipation of the end of the trend.

Ginsberg noted that Durkheim's evidence for the relationship between the suicide rate and the economy was poor. First it was selective. Secondly, he produced no evidence for a crisis of prosperity. He showed that the suicide rate was high when there were many bankruptcies, but he did not look at times when there were few. Thirdly, he looked at long-term trends and not crises. However, Ginsberg's own arguments appear to have post hoc elements, and we shall try to illustrate this.

Ginsberg noted that, if an increase in business prosperity stops early (before the natural peak is reached), a large gap between aspiration level and rewards will occur compared to what happens when the increase follows the usual course. Thus there will be an increase in the suicide rate just before the peak of business prosperity for slow rises in business prosperity, just as Henry and Short found (see Chapter 5).

Similarly a decrease in business prosperity that stops early should lead to a decrease in the suicide rate just before the trough of business prosperity is reached. Ginsberg, however, did not predict this. Instead he predicted that, in sharp downswings, the level of aspiration almost catches up with rewards, eliminating dissatisfaction and leading to a reduced suicide rate. In slow downswings, the aspiration level does not catch up with the decreasing rewards, and so the suicide rate increases. Thus Ginsberg's argument here does not parallel his argument for similar situations regarding business upswings. There appears to be a degree of arbitrariness in Ginsberg's choice of arguments and furthermore it is not always clear that his prediction is the only one possible given his set of assumptions.

It should be noted that Ginsberg differs from Durkheim in many respects, among which one of the most important is that, for Durkheim, anomie necessarily involved unlimited aspirations, whereas for Ginsberg the anomic process need not involve unlimited aspirations.

Before we leave Ginsberg's ideas, it is of interest to note his conceptualization of the idea of *fatalism*. Fatalism, for Ginsberg, involved these factors: (a) a gap between aspirations and reward, (b) the aspirations are within the interval of distributive justice, (c) the rewards are low and outside of the interval of distributive justice, that is, illegitimate, and (d) since the rewards are illegitimate, the outcomes are independent of the way an individual feels and acts. Ginsberg did follow Durkheim in seeing normative control as excessive in fatalism (point c) but absent in anomie.

Discussion

We will present a formal economic model of Ginsberg's theory in Chapter 6 but, to anticipate, the theory predicts a positive association between economic prosperity and the suicide rate. It is important to note that Ginsberg did not attempt to test his theory empirically. We shall explore in

Part 4 of this book the extent to which the observed associations do indeed fit his theory.

REFERENCES

Ginsberg, R. B. Anomie and aspirations. *Dissertation Abstracts*, 1966, 27A, 3945-3946.

March, J., & Simon, H. *Organizations*. New York: Wiley, 1958.

CHAPTER 5

HENRY AND SHORT

After Durkheim's (1897) theory of suicide, the next major contribution to the sociological study of suicide was made by Andrew Henry and James Short (1954). Their work is unusual in that it draws together a number of themes in both sociology and psychology. The concepts of social integration and social regulation proposed by Durkheim remain important. However, Henry and Short brought in the psychoanalytic ideas of Freud as well.

In an early version of psychoanalytic theory, Freud proposed that the primary response to frustration was aggression directed outwardly toward the person or object frustrating the child (Lester, 1987). This automatic response was inhibited by the child's parents during the process of socializing the child. If this outwardly aggressive response is severely inhibited, the child probably will mature into a depressed and suicidal person. Thus, suicide and homicide, for Henry and Short, were opposed behaviors. Correlates of suicidal behavior were, on the whole, expected to be opposite from those of homicidal behavior, and this hypothesis has been explored extensively (Lester, 1987).

Henry and Short's adoption of this Freudian hypothesis led them to consider usefulness of the frustration-aggression hypothesis, proposed by Dollard, et al. (1939), in furthering our understanding of suicide and homicide.

Henry and Short, therefore, ended by proposing social determinants *and* psychological determinants of the choice of the direction for the expression of the aggression that follows frustration. They also spent consid-

erable time in their book exploring the relationship between business prosperity and depression to suicide and homicide and interpreting their findings in the framework of these theories.

Let us first review briefly their research on suicide, homicide and the
business cycle.

SUICIDE, HOMICIDE AND THE ECONOMY

In their investigation of the relationship between the business cycle and
suicide and homicide rates, Henry and Short made two major predictions:
(a) Suicide rates will rise during times of business depression and fall
during times of business prosperity, while crimes of violence against people will rise during business prosperity and fall during business depressions, and (b) the correlation between suicide rates and the business cycle
will be higher for high status groups than for low status groups, while the
correlation between homicide rates and the business cycle will be higher
for low status groups than for high status groups.

The results which Henry and Short presented partially supported their
predictions. The only status categories with data available for both suicide
and homicide rates was that of whites and nonwhites. The correlations
between suicide and homicide rates and the business cycle (measured by
the Ayres Index of Industrial Activity) during the period including 1900 to
1947 were:

	whites	nonwhites
suicide	-0.81	-0.38
homicide	-0.51	0.49

Although Henry and Short were not able to use rates with which people
murdered others for whites and nonwhites, they argued that most murders
were intra-racial, and so the homicide rates for white and nonwhite victims
were good approximations of the rate with each racial group murdered.

The second prediction (point b above) was confirmed (though we should note that Henry and Short did not carry out any statistical tests of significance on their data). The negative correlation between suicide rates and the business cycle was greater for the high status group (whites) than it was for the low status group (blacks), whereas the positive correlation between homicide rates and the business cycle was higher for the low status group than for the high status group. However, the first prediction (point a above) was not confirmed. The prediction of a positive correlation between homicide rates and the business cycle was not found for whites. It must be concluded that the results only partially confirmed their predictions. (It should be noted that the population base for suicide and homicide rates in the United States changed up to 1933, after which the full United States reported deaths to the federal government. Thus, Henry and Short's analyses were based on a changing population base.)

Henry and Short reported a variety of other phenomena.

(1) Suicide rates increased in 82 percent of the years in which the Ayres' Index was falling, but decreased in only 58 percent of the years in which the index was rising.

(2) Suicide rates reached their peak in the same year in which the business index reached a trough, but suicide rates reached their trough a year or two before the business index reached its peak.

(3) Henry and Short predicted that the association between the suicide rate and the business cycle would be stronger for men than for women because of the differences in their status. The difference was in the predicted direction, though small: -0.76 for men and -0.71 for women.

(4) The association between the suicide rate and the business cycle was stronger for both men and women of working age (15 to 65) than for those over the age of 65.

FRUSTRATION, AGGRESSION, AND THE BUSINESS CYCLE

Henry and Short interpreted their results in terms of the frustration-aggression hypothesis (Dollard, et al., 1939). Their assumptions were (a) aggression is often a consequence of frustration, (b) business cycles produce variations in the hierarchical rankings of persons by status, and (c) frustrations are generated by a failure to maintain a constant or rising position in the status hierarchy relative to the status position of other groups.

The interpretation of their results required two additional assumptions: (a) high status persons lose status relative to low status persons during business contraction while low status persons lose status relative to high status persons during business expansions, and (b) suicide occurs mainly in high status persons while homicide occurs mainly in low status persons.

Consider those who lose income during business contraction. The higher status person has more income to lose, and his fall is greater than that of the low status person. The high status person loses status relative to the low status person. The low status person may actually experience a gain in status relative to the high status person. Thus in times of business contraction, high status people lose status relative to low status people, and this generates frustration. The aggression consequent to this frustration in high status people is predominantly self-directed aggression, and so suicide rates rise in times of business contraction in high status people. This analysis explains why suicide rates and the business cycle are negatively correlated in whites, a high status group.

Henry and Short extended their analysis by considering high and low class whites and high and low class blacks. If suicide occurs mainly in high status whites and blacks, then why should the correlation between the business cycle and suicide rates be larger in whites than in blacks? Henry and Short predicted this difference since whites are of higher status than blacks and high class whites are of higher status than high class blacks.

This analysis raises problems. For example, consider homicide. During business contraction, lower class whites lose status relative to lower class blacks. Therefore, they will suffer frustration, and the aggression consequent to this frustration will be homicide since they are low status people. Thus their homicide rate should increase during business contraction -- or so Henry and Short argued. But their status relative to high class whites rises during business contraction and thus their homicide rates should decrease. Which analysis is correct? Is there a rule for deciding which analysis is correct? No.

When all of these explanations are considered together, it becomes clear that Henry and Short have assumed that whites assess their relative status by comparing themselves to blacks and vice versa, that high class whites assess their status relative to low class whites and vice versa, and that high class blacks assess their status relative to low class blacks and vice versa. The first of these assumptions is incompatible with the latter two. Do high class blacks assess their status relative to low or high class whites or blacks? Henry and Short assume, for example, that when a black is considered as a black, he assesses his status relative to whites, but that when he is considered as a high class black he assesses his status relative to low class blacks. This makes less than good sense. A person's assessment of himself is independent of how we may choose to label him.

So, Henry and Short changed the reference groups for particular groups of individuals in order to account for the particular associations that arise. There is no general rule possible to decide which reference group a particular societal subgroup will choose, whether it will be within racial groups or across racial groups for example. The system becomes, therefore, post hoc. The reference groups are deduced after the correlations between the suicide and homicide rates and the business cycle have been determined.

Discussion

Henry and Short's theory of the relationship between the business cycle and suicide has been quite successful in accounting for some of the research findings. The fact that part of their reasoning is post hoc detracts from the adequacy of their presentation, but future theorists may be able to predict the research results without such logical errors.

Henry and Short's theory also broadened our perspective by suggesting that homicide should be studied as well as suicide in order to provide a clearer picture of the relationship between business activity and aggressive behavior. They also integrated sociological and psychological insights into suicide, a task not seriously attempted by other theorists.

To anticipate Chapter 6 where we present a formal model of their theory, Henry and Short's theory predicts that suicide and the business cycle are related by a monotonic negative function. Suicide rates and the business cycle are, on the whole, negatively associated.

REFERENCES

Dollard, J., Doob, L., Miller, N., Mowrer, O. H., & Sears, R. *Frustration and aggression*. New Haven: Yale University Press, 1939.

Durkheim, E. *Le suicide*. Paris: Felix Alcan, 1897.

Henry, A. F., & Short, J. F. *Suicide and homicide*. New York: Free Press, 1954.

Lester, D. Murders and suicide: are they polar opposites? *Behavioral Sciences & the Law*, 1987, 5, 49-60.

CHAPTER 6

FORMAL MODELS OF THE ECONOMY AND SUICIDE

In the previous chapters, we have presented three theories (from Durkheim, Ginsberg, and Henry and Short) of how the economy might be related to suicidal behavior. Words can have ambiguous meanings, and our intent in the present chapter is to translate these three theories into functional form so that such ambiguities may be avoided.

DURKHEIM'S U-SHAPED THEORY

The basic tenet in Durkheim's (1897) sociological explanation of suicide can be summarized by the following equations.

(1) $S = f(SI, SR)$

(2) $SI = g(y)$

(3) $SR = h(y)$

(4) $y = \hat{y} - \hat{y}^*$

where
    S is the suicide rate
    SI is the social integration index
    SR is the social regulation index
    y is the business cycle index
    $\hat{y}$ is the actual economic growth rate
    $\hat{y}^*$ is the potential economic growth rate
    f, g, and h are functions

Equation (1) states Durkheim's fundamental idea that suicide reflects the extent of the social integration and social regulation in a society. Equations (2) and (3) indicate respectively that both social integration and social regulation are related to the business cycle. The business cycle index y is defined as the departure of the actual economic growth rate from the potential economic growth rate. When y > 0, the economy is expanding, whereas when y < 0 the economy is contracting.

Durkheim assumed that

(i) $\dfrac{\partial f}{\partial SI} < 0,\ \dfrac{\partial f}{\partial SR} < 0$

(ii) $\dfrac{dg}{d\,|\,y\,|} < 0,\ \dfrac{dh}{d\,|\,y\,|} < 0$

where |y| refers to the absolute value of y. This means, (i) the higher the social integration and social regulation, the lower the suicide rate, and (ii) the greater the economic expansion and recession, the less social integration and regulation there will be. In order to obtain the impact of the business cycle on suicide, we differentiate S with respect to |y| as follows.

$$\frac{ds}{d\,|\,y\,|} = \frac{\partial f}{\partial SI} \cdot \frac{dg}{d\,|\,y\,|} + \frac{\partial f}{\partial SR} \cdot \frac{dh}{d\,|\,y\,|}$$

Based on assumptions (i) and (ii), we can conclude that

(5) $\dfrac{ds}{d\,|\,y\,|} > 0$

Thus, the more the economy expands or contracts, the higher the suicide rate.

If we draw a diagram using the vertical axis to indicate the suicide rate and the horizontal axis to indicate the business cycle index, then Durkheim's theory of suicide and the business cycle will be a pointed V-shaped curve intersecting the vertical axis at a level indicating a minimum possible suicide rate (see Figure 6.1).

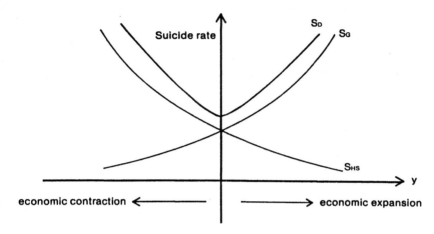

SD   the suicide rate as a function of the business cycle for Durkheim
SG   the suicide rate as a function of the business cycle for Ginsburg
SHS   the suicide rate as a function of the business cycle for Henry and Short
Y   the business cycle index

Figure 6.1 The Three Models of Suicide and the Business Cycle

GINSBERG'S PROCYCLICAL THEORY

Ginsberg (1966) noted that suicide arose from the dissatisfaction of individuals. Dissatisfaction itself was related directly to the discrepancy between the actual reward that the individual was receiving and his level of aspiration. Ginsberg assumed that the actual reward varies positively with the business cycle.

These formulations can be applied to the society as a whole by replacing the individual level of dissatisfaction, reward, and aspiration with the average level for the society as a whole. The formulations can then be summarized as follows:

(6) $S = f(D), \dfrac{ds}{dD} > 0$

(7) $D = g(A/R), \dfrac{\partial D}{\partial A} > 0, \dfrac{\partial D}{\partial R} < 0$

(8) $R = h(y), \dfrac{dR}{dy} > 0$

(9) $A = k(R), \dfrac{dA}{dR} > 0$

(10) If $\dfrac{d^2 R}{dt^2} > 0$, *then* $\dfrac{d^2 A}{dt^2} = \beta \dfrac{d^2 R}{dt^2}$, $\beta > 0$

(11) If $\dfrac{d^2 R}{dt^2} < 0$, *then* $\left| \dfrac{d^2 A}{dt^2} \right| > \left| \dfrac{d^2 R}{dt^2} \right|$

where
  S is the suicide rate
  D is the average level of dissatisfaction of the society
  A is the average level of aspiration of the society
  R is the average reward received by people in the society
  $\frac{dx}{dt}$ is the rate of change of any variable x over time
  $\frac{d^2 x}{dt^2}$ is the rate of change of $\frac{dx}{dt}$ over time
  β is a constant

Equation (6) states that the suicide rate is directly related to the society's level of dissatisfaction. Equation (7) formulates Ginsberg's idea that, if the average level of a society's aspiration changes at a faster rate than the average level of reward, then the result is an increase in the society's level of dissatisfaction. This also explains the signs of the partial derivatives of both variables. Equation (8) specifies how the level of reward is determined. The greater the economic expansion, the higher the rewards, and vice versa. Equation (9) indicates that the aspiration level is a positive function of the rate of change in the level of rewards, that is, if the level of rewards keeps increasing, the level of aspiration will rise accordingly, and vice versa.

Lastly, equations (10) and (11) dictate the variation of the level of aspiration over time as a function of the change in the rate of change of the level of rewards. Equation (10) states that, whenever the rate of increase in the level of rewards changes (increases or decreases) at an increasing rate, the level of aspiration will vary directly with the level of rewards. Equation (11) postulates that, if the rate of change of the level of rewards changes at a decreasing rate, then the rate of change of the level of aspiration will change at a faster rate than the rate of change of the level of rewards.[1]

Based on these formulations and assumptions, the suicide rate should be a positive function of the business cycle index. In other words, the total differential of S with respect to y should be as follows:

$$\frac{ds}{dy} = \frac{df}{dD} \cdot \frac{\partial D}{\partial R} \cdot \frac{dR}{dy} + \frac{df}{dD} \cdot \frac{\partial D}{\partial A} \cdot \frac{dA}{dy} = \frac{df}{dD}\left[\frac{\partial D}{\partial R} \cdot \frac{dR}{dy} + \frac{\partial D}{\partial A} \cdot \frac{dA}{dy}\right]$$

According to the principles postulated in equations (10) and (11), the impact of the economic condition on the level of aspiration will be greater than on the level of rewards, that is,

$$\left|\frac{\partial D}{\partial A} \cdot \frac{dA}{dy}\right| > \left|\frac{\partial D}{\partial R} \cdot \frac{dR}{dy}\right|$$

With $\frac{df}{dD} > 0$, $\frac{dA}{dy} > 0$, $\frac{dR}{dy} > 0$, $\frac{\partial D}{\partial A} > 0$, and $\frac{\partial D}{\partial R} < 0$

---

[1] The rate of variation of the levels of aspiration and rewards is indicated by the differentiation of the variable with respect to time for the sake of simplicity. Presumably they are driven by the cyclical business activity as postulated by Ginsberg.

this implies that $\dfrac{ds}{dy} > 0$ (see footnote [2])

When the economy is expanding, the level of rewards in the society also grows, as does the level of aspirations, and so also will the suicide rate. If the economy keeps its growth momentum, then the level of aspirations will rise at a faster rate than will the level of rewards. Therefore, the suicide rate will also rise due to the growing level of anomic dissatisfaction as a result of the increasing disparity of aspirations from rewards. However, this is true before the economy reaches its peak of economic expansion because, as the economy nears the peak, there is a slowdown in the rate of expansion.

By the same token, when the economy is running into a recession, the rate of aspiration is decreasing because the level of rewards is decreasing. As the economy approaches the trough, the rate of decline of the economy slows down, the level of aspiration decreases at faster rate than the level of rewards, and the discrepancy between the levels of reward and aspiration shrinks. This leads to a lower level of societal dissatisfaction and ultimately a lower suicide rate. It should be noted that the declining suicide rate will reverse near the trough of the business cycle.

In summary, the suicide rate as a function of the business cycle should be an upward-sloping curve except at the extremes of the business cycle (the peaks and the troughs) as shown in Figure 6.1. Interestingly, the conclusions drawn by Ginsberg for recessions indicate that the declining sui-

---

[2] Among those inequalities,

$$\frac{dt}{dD} > 0, \ \frac{dR}{dy} > 0, \ \frac{\partial D}{\partial A} > 0, \ and \ \frac{\partial D}{\partial R} < 0$$

are in accordance with equations (6), (7) and (8), whereas $\dfrac{dA}{dy}$ can be derived as follows:

$$\frac{dA}{dy} = \frac{dK}{dR} \cdot \frac{dR}{dy} \ [\ because \ A = k(R) \ ]$$

As $\dfrac{dk}{dR}$ and $\dfrac{dR}{dy}$ are positive, according to equations (8) and (9), therefore, $\dfrac{dA}{dy} > 0$

cide rate occurs only as a special case of sharp downswings (Lester, 1972, p. 85).[3]

HENRY AND SHORT'S COUNTERCYCLICAL THEORY

Henry and Short's (1954) prediction of the relationship between the business cycle and suicide is that suicide rates are countercyclical. That is, suicide rates tend to fall during times of business prosperity and rise during times of business depression. They interpreted this relationship in terms of the frustration-aggression hypothesis.

Henry and Short established their hypothesis on the basis of the following assumptions: (i) frustration often results in aggression, (ii) business cycles affect the hierarchical rankings of persons by status, (iii) frustrations are caused by a failure to maintain a constant or rising position in the status hierarchy relative to the status position of other groups, (iv) high status persons lose status relative to low status persons during business contraction, while they gain relative status during business expansion, and (v) suicide occurs mainly in high status persons.

Following these assumptions, Henry and Short's model includes the following equations and one inequality:

(12) $S = f(RS)$, $f' = \dfrac{df}{dRS} < 0$

(13) $RS = E_H / E_L$

(14) $E_H = g(y)$, $g' = \dfrac{dE_H}{dy} > 0$

(15) $E_L = h(y)$, $h' = \dfrac{dE_L}{dy} > 0$

(16) $g'/E_H > h'/E_L$

---

[3] Even though Ginsberg claimed that the declining suicide rate during recessions was a special case of his theory, his theory seems to imply that only the declining suicide rate during recession is consistent with the principles postulated in equations (10) and (11).

where
S is the suicide rate
RS is the relative status of high status persons
E_H is the hierarchical position of the high status persons
E_L is the hierarchical position of the low status persons
y is the business cycle index

Equations (12) and (13) together state that suicide is negatively related to the relative status of the high status persons, with their relative status defined as the ratio of the hierarchical position of the high status persons to that of the other groups. The higher the ratio, the less frustration the high status persons tend to feel and the lower the suicide rate.

Equations (14) and (15) indicate that the hierarchical position of both high status and low status persons should rise or fall with business expansions or contractions. However, the degree of impact of the business cycle on both groups is different as shown by equation (16). The impact of the business cycle on the high status groups is greater than on the other groups. This is why, when the economy expands, the high status group's hierarchical position improves relatively more than that of the other groups whereas, when the economy contracts, the high status group's hierarchical position worsens relatively more than that of the other groups. As a consequence, the suicide rate shows a negative relationship with the business cycle index.

This conclusion may be derived by differentiating the suicide rate with respect to the business cycle index.

$$\frac{ds}{dy} = \frac{dS}{dRS} \cdot \frac{\partial RS}{\partial E_H} \cdot \frac{dE_H}{dy} + \frac{dS}{dRS} \cdot \frac{\partial RS}{\partial E_L} \frac{dE_l}{dy}$$

$$= f^1 \left[\frac{1}{E_L} g^1 - \frac{E_H}{E_L^2} h^1 \right]$$

$$= RSf^1 \left[\frac{g^1}{E_H} - \frac{h^1}{E_L} \right]$$

With equations (12) and (16), plus RS > 0, this implies that $\frac{ds}{dy} < 0$

Henry and Short's countercyclical theory of suicide is depicted by a downward sloping curve in Figure 6.1.

EMPIRICAL TESTS OF THE THEORIES

Surprisingly, there have not been many tests of these three alternative theories. There has, of course, been a great deal of empirical research into the relationship between economic variables and the suicide rate, and we will review this research in Part 4 of this book. However, that research has rarely been designed to test which of the three theories reviewed in this section is valid. For example, to explore whether suicidal behavior is more common in those who are unemployed than in those who are employed is of great interest, but it does not formally test the three theories.

The first major test of the three theories was published by Pierce (1967) who examined the suicide rate in the United States from 1919 to 1940. Pierce examined several economic indicators, including the Ayres index of industrial activity, relative income, the unemployment rate, and the construction of new dwelling units. He also examined the effects of using absolute values of the economic indicators versus year-to-year differences, linear, exponential and polynomial regression, and various lags between the economic indicators and age-standardized suicide rates of white males.

He concluded that year-to-year differences in the economic indicators made better theoretical sense than the use of absolute levels, and that the public's definition of the economic situation would be the best economic indicator. Consequently, "the absolute values of the first differences of the index of common stock prices were correlated by a one-year lead with the suicide rates" (Pierce, 1967, p. 461). We quote the exact words used by Pierce since he has been extensively criticized for his methodology. He found a correlation of 0.74, accounting for 55 percent of the variance in the suicide rates. Taking into account the direction of the differences reduced the size of the correlation to -0.49. Pierce concluded that his results supported Durkheim's hypothesis that economic change, regardless of its direction, led to increased suicide rates, and failed to confirm Henry and Short's hypothesis.

Marshall and Hodge (1981) criticized Pierce's study. First, only after 1933 did all states report mortality statistics to the federal government. Thus, the time period should be from 1933 on. Marshall and Hodge also claimed that Pierce used negative time lags, that is, he compared the economic variable in year t with the suicide rate in year (t-1), resulting in "nonsense" correlations. If Marshall and Hodge are correct, then Pierce's study is indeed faulty. However, if we examine the exact wording used by Pierce in his critical correlation and quoted above, it is by no means clear that Marshall and Hodge's interpretation is correct.

Marshall and Hodge also suggested the usefulness of a multiple regression analysis. They hypothesized that changes in the suicide rate would be a linear function of:

1. the state of the economy (the unemployment rate)

2. economic improvement or deterioration (the first difference in the yearly stock market price)

3. economic change (the absolute value of the first difference in the yearly stock market price)

4. and the pre-existing level of suicide.

Examining the United States from 1933 to 1976, Marshall and Hodge found that three of these variables were significant in the multiple regression, the pre-existing suicide rate and the unemployment rate positively and the first difference in the yearly stock market price negatively.

Marshall and Hodge argued, therefore, that the importance of the absolute magnitude of change was not supported by their data. Rather, economic hardship appeared to be related to suicide as Henry and Short's theory would predict. Suicide rates are higher when unemployment rates are higher and when there are negative changes in the economy.

Reflection on these two studies shows that neither measured economic expansion and contraction adequately, and neither made an attempt to geometrically plot the suicide rate against economic change. What would happen if we attempted this? We plotted the year-to-year percentage change in the gross national product (in constant 1982 dollars) against the suicide rate of the United States from 1933 to 1986 -- see Figure 6.2. It is clear that there was no association.

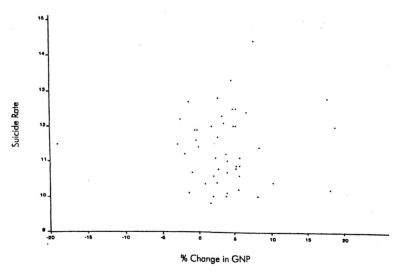

Figure 6.2 The Suicide Rate and the Business Cycle, 1933-1986

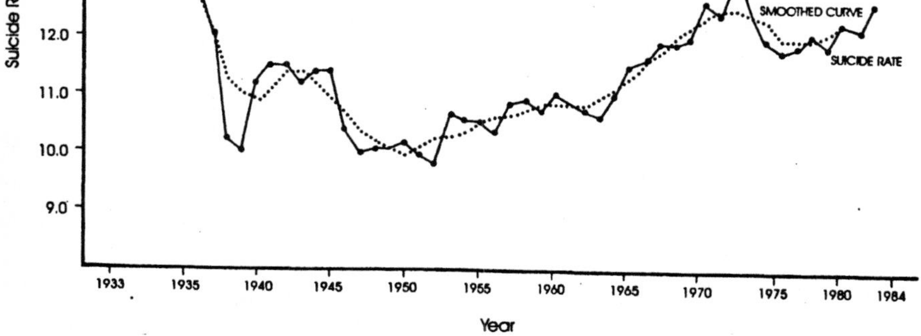

Figure 6.3 The Yearly Suicide Rate and the Five-Year Moving Average

We also plotted the year-to-year percentage change in the gross national product against the signed difference between the suicide rate each year and the five-year moving average of the suicide rate. The suicide rate changes over time in the United States, and a five year moving average identifies the long-term trend, around which there are yearly fluctuations -- see Figure 6.3. Our second plot examined whether economic expansion and contraction was related to the size of these yearly fluctuations. The result is shown in Figures 6.4 and 6.5.

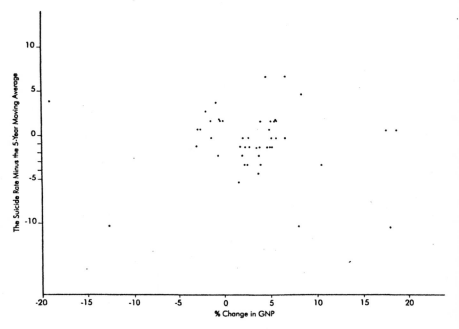

Figure 6.4 The Business Cycle and Fluctuations in the Suicide Rate, 1933-1986

Figure 6.4 includes all of the data points, and examination of the cloud of points suggests a V-shaped function. To heighten this, we averaged the data points within each unit of economic change -- see Figure 6.5. Now the V-shaped function is clearer. Extreme economic changes, both expansions and contractions, in the United States during this period were associated

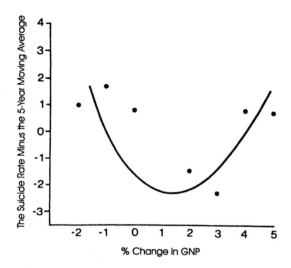

Figure 6.5 The Business Cycle and Fluctuations in the Suicide Rate-Averages

with increases in the actual suicide rate over the long-term trend. These data, therefore, support Durkheim.

It is safe to say, however, that the debate will continue in the future, and hopefully in a few years we will be able to evaluate the three theories more adequately.

DISCUSSION

While Durkheim claimed that suicide rates tend to climb during times of economic expansion and contraction, Ginsberg argued that suicide rates should rise only in times of economic expansion while dropping during times of economic recession. In contrast, Henry and Short argued that suicide rates rise only during economic contraction but not in times of economic expansion. Despite these differences, these three theories share several features in common.

First, the suicide rate is related to the business cycle. Therefore, the suicide rate should be a function of the economic activity of the entire community.

Second, even though they all recognized the driving force of the economy behind the suicide rate, this force was mediated through other variables. In Durkheim's case, the mediating variables are social integration and social regulation. In Ginsberg's case, the mediating variable is aspirations relative to actual rewards received. In Henry and Short's case, the mediating variable is the relative status of social groups. This feature may be used to justify the assumption that economic variables *cannot* be treated as the single force that "causes everything to happen. All social and political life waits for the economy to tell it what to do" (Marshall and Hodge, 1981, p. 107). It seems more likely that *both* social variables and economic variables play a role in the determination of the suicide rate of a society.

Third, even though the rise and fall of the suicide rate as a function of the economy is different in each theory, all the theories predict that the curve intersects the vertical axis at a certain level during normal economic conditions. This seems to imply that for every society there is some inevitable minimum suicide rate. We may call this the *natural suicide rate*. These sociological theories imply that this rate is greater than zero.

REFERENCES

Durkheim, E. *Le suicide*. Paris: Felix Alcan, 1897.

Ginsberg, R. B. Anomie and aspirations. *Dissertation Abstracts*, 1966, 27A, 3945-3946.

Henry, A. F., & Short, J. F. *Suicide and homicide*. New York: Free Press, 1954.

Marshall, J. R., & Hodge, R. W. Durkheim and Pierce on suicide and economic change. *Social Science Research*, 1981, 10, 101-114.

Pierce, A. The economic cycle and the social suicide rate. *American Sociological Review*, 1967, 32, 457-462.

Part 3:

Economic Models of Suicide

CHAPTER 7

A DEMAND AND SUPPLY MODEL OF SUICIDE

The similarity between the analysis of some issues in economics and related issues in psychology has often been noted. For example, Lea (1978) has noted that both economics and psychology are concerned with choices, and some of the basic assumptions of theories of choice are common to both disciplines.

In particular, Lea noted that analogies exist between the paradigm of operant conditioning in psychology and demand analysis in economics. Economists call the function which relates the quantity of a commodity that is bought by a consumer to the price of the commodity the *demand curve*. Lea argued that the number of reinforcements obtained in operant conditioning is equivalent to the "quantity bought" by a subject. The schedule of reinforcement is equivalent to the "price." The schedule of reinforcement may be fixed-interval or fixed-ratio, and the variation in the size of the schedule (which interval or which ratio) parallels the price.

Lester (1988) has proposed a learning theory for suicide. He argued that suicide is, at least in part, a learned behavior, and he documented how this might be so. He examined the role that cultural norms, childhood experiences of punishment, and the rewards contingent upon self-harming behavior play in determining the occurrence of suicidal behavior. His analysis suggested to us that an economic model of suicide might be possible since learning theory and demand analysis in economics share similarities, as Lea pointed out.

The purpose of this chapter then is to propose an economic model of suicidal behavior based on economic concepts.

A Cost-Benefit Analysis of Suicide

In a cost-benefit analysis of suicide, committing suicide is considered to be a rational act. An individual is acting "rationally" if, given a choice between various alternatives, he selects what seems to be the most desirable or the least undesirable alternative. Economists would not judge whether suicide is a wrong, immoral, or deviant act.

The decision to commit suicide depends upon the benefits and costs associated with suicide and with alternative actions. An individual will be less likely to commit suicide if the benefits from suicide decrease, the costs of suicide increase, the costs of alternative actions decrease, or the benefits from alternative activities increase.

The benefits from suicide include escape from physical or psychological pain (as in the suicide of someone dying from terminal cancer), the anticipation of the impact of the suicide's death on other people (as in someone who hopes to make the survivors feel guilty), or restoring one's public image (as in the suicide of Antigone in Sophocles' play of the same name). In addition, the act itself may be enjoyable. Those who self-injure themselves by cutting their wrists sometimes report that the act of cutting relieves built-up tension and that they feel no pain.

There are several costs in committing suicide. These include the money and effort spent in obtaining the information and equipment needed for the act of suicide, the pain involved in preparing to kill oneself and in the process of committing suicide, the expected loss as a result of committing suicide such as the expected punishment predicted by most of the major religions of the world, and the opportunity costs (that is, the net gain to be expected if other alternative activities were chosen and life continued).

An individual will engage in suicide only if its benefits are greater than all of the costs mentioned above. Therefore, our economic model would suggest preventing suicide by increasing its costs or by decreasing its benefits.

A DEMAND AND SUPPLY ANALYSIS OF SUICIDE

In this section we will examine suicide as if it were a commodity or a service that we buy. However, it is immediately obvious that suicide is very different from the typical objects that we purchase. For example, when we buy an object, we pay a specific price to obtain it and then we enjoy it. Suicide results in death, and as a result we have to conceptualize our enjoyment of it quite differently.

Suicide is somewhat similar to the purchasing of health care services. In both, we pay a price to get rid of something, life in the case of suicide and sickness in the case of health care. Yet there is a basic difference between suicide and health care in that suicide leads to death, while health care (hopefully) leads to further life. Of course, for those who believe that there will be a "life-after-death," suicide also leads to further life, but of a different kind.

Looking at matters from a demand side perspective, when we purchase a commodity (or a service), the price we pay for the commodity (or service) reflects the benefits we expect to receive from consuming that commodity. From a demand side perspective, beef costs more than chicken because the public desires beef more, and their stronger desire for beef reflects their expectation of greater satisfaction from eating beef than from eating chicken.

In a demand side analysis of suicide, the notion of its "price" is different from the ordinary price of a commodity. The benefit expected by a suicide is the relief of tremendous distress. Accordingly, we must use a scale of distress to measure the benefit expected by the suicidal individual. This benefit expected by the suicidal individual is reflected in the price he must pay for his suicide.

Accordingly the demand curve is a relationship indicating the probability of committing suicide as a function of the amount of distress felt by the individual. As the amount of distress increases, the probability of committing suicide increases. The demand for suicide is, therefore, an upward sloping curve, which is quite different from the typical downward sloping demand curve found in most economic analyses.

On the supply side, the probability of committing suicide is related to the cost of committing suicide. The cost of committing suicide includes the cost of losing your life, collecting information about how to commit the act, purchasing the means for suicide, etc. While the latter two items have a clear-cut scale of measurement, the cost of losing life is much harder to measure. It includes at least three components, namely, the psychological fear of death, the loss of income in the future which otherwise would have been earned by the suicide, and the loss of any enjoyment that would be experienced during the rest of your "natural" life.

The higher the cost of committing suicide, the lower the probability that an individual will actually kill himself. Therefore, the supply curve should be a downward sloping curve.

Both the demand for suicide and supply for suicide are shown in Figure 7.1. The vertical axis indicates the price (or the cost) of committing suicide, while the horizontal axis represents the probability of committing suicide. Since the probability of committing suicide is used to indicate the quantity demanded or supplied, the upper limit for this variable is one. The demand

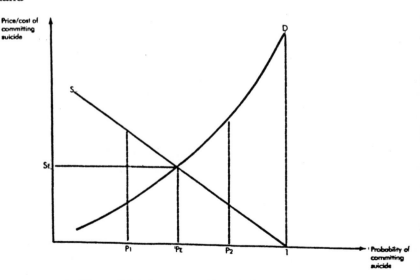

Figure 7.1 A Demand and Supply Curve for Suicide

curve is an upward sloping curve and becomes vertical when the probability of committing suicide is equal to one. The price level for committing suicide, which corresponds to the point where the probability is equal to one, refers to the threshold level of distress that an individual can no longer tolerate. In this situation, committing suicide becomes inevitable.

The intersection of the demand and supply curves represents an equilibrium for an individual. For that equilibrium level of distress and the corresponding costs of committing suicide, there is an equilibrium probability of committing suicide. As the supply curve might intersect any section of the demand curve, the equilibrium probability of committing suicide can range anywhere from zero to one.

What needs to be determined in this demand-supply analysis of suicide is how to convert the psychological variables (level of distress and future pleasure) into measures comparable to monetary units, so that an equilibrium can be obtained through equating the demand and supply for suicide.

One way to measure the level of distress is to operationalize it as the cost of the psychological services required to eliminate the distress that the suicidal person is experiencing. Since there is a typical price for psychological services, each level of distress could be converted into a monetary measure representing the cost of psychological services needed to eliminate the distress.

This is complicated by the fact that psychological services are not always effective. Some people do not benefit from treatment. This could be taken into account by incorporating the probability of success of the treatment into the calculations, as a multiplier of the cost of treatment.

Converting future pleasure from life into monetary units is more difficult. One alternative could be to convert all of the components of the cost into subjective units, based on the ratings given by representative members of the society.

INSTABILITY OF SUICIDAL BEHAVIOR

By definition, the equilibrium probability of committing suicide is determined by the intersection of the supply and demand curves. Due to the peculiar nature of the demand and supply of suicide, the equilibrium so obtained is not a stable one.

Since the demand for suicide is an upward sloping line, the higher the distress level, the more likely the probability of committing suicide. Since the supply curve is downward sloping, the higher the cost of committing suicide, the less likely the probability of doing so. Let us label the equilibrium level of distress and the cost of committing suicide S_E and the corresponding equilibrium probability P_E (see Figure 7.1).

Let us examine the implications of these supply and demand curves. If the probability of committing suicide is initially at P_1, which is lower than the equilibrium probability P_E, this corresponds to a low level of distress from the demand side perspective and a high cost of committing suicide from the supply side perspective (see Figure 7.1). As a result, the situation will lead to an even lower probability of committing suicide, and the individual will eventually withdraw from the suicidal situation.

Table 7.1 Suicide rates in the United States by method per 100,000 people per year

	total suicide rate	firearm suicide rate	non-firearm suicide rate
1960	10.6	5.0	5.6
1970	11.6	5.8	5.8
1980	11.9	6.8	5.1
1990	12.4	7.5	4.9

On the other hand, if the probability of committing suicide initially is higher than the equilibrium probability P_E, say at P_2, this corresponds to a high level of distress from the demand side perspective and a low cost of committing suicide from a supply side perspective (see Figure 7.1). Thus, this situation will lead to an even higher probability of committing suicide.

Both situations, whether the initial probability of committing suicide is higher or lower than the equilibrium, result in movement away from the equilibrium. If the initial probability of committing suicide is lower than the equilibrium, then the individual becomes less likely to commit suicide; while if the initial probability of committing suicide is higher than the equilibrium the individual becomes more likely to commit suicide. In short, this economic model of suicide implies that suicidal behavior is an unstable behavior.

FACTORS BEHIND THE SUPPLY AND DEMAND FOR SUICIDE

What are the factors that contribute to the decision to commit suicide? There are many factors involved (Lester, 1983), but the primary ones include personality, education, age, sex, family background, and social environment.

Among the research conducted into the personality of suicidal people, the most promising variables identified so far are self-esteem and psychiatric disturbance. Several studies have also suggested that suicidal people are introverted and may have a belief in an external locus of control, but the research is inconsistent for these variables (Lester, 1983).

There is evidence that less educated people are more likely to complete suicide than the more educated (Kitagawa and Hauser, 1973). Completed suicide rates typically rise with age, and there is a clear sex difference in suicidal behavior, in which males complete suicide at a higher rate while females attempt suicide at a higher rate (Lester, 1979).

Family background includes such variables as genes, race, social class, single-parenthood, etc. Whether the family provides a loving environment should be an important factor too, but this might be difficult to quantify. Included in the family background is family income (financial status). For example, Barnes (1975) found that the completed suicide rate of adult white males in different regions of the United States was related to the family income of white families.

The social environment also includes many economic variables. Stack (1978, 1979) looked at the suicide rate of nations of the world as related to their gross national product per capita, female participation in the labor force, rate of economic growth, population density, and political totalitarianism.

There is one factor that might fall into both family and social sets of variables -- the incidence of suicide in the social networks of the individual, both in the family and outside the family. According to a social learning theory of suicide, the individual might form and develop the idea of committing suicide because it has been modeled by one or more of his/her family members, peer group friends, or mentors. If the potential suicide picks up the idea for suicide from his social network, then the demand curve for suicide will shift to the right, indicating a much higher probability of suicide whatever the cost of suicide might be.

Most of the factors mentioned so far are those which shed some light on the determination of the demand for suicide, since the supply curve is a function of the costs of committing suicide.

One common feature shared by all of these demand-side variables is that they are reasonably stable characteristics. Once the demand curve is formed, it remains quite stable over time. Sudden shifts of the demand curve would be caused by events such as sudden deaths in the family, marital disruptions, changing jobs, etc. The extent to which the demand curve shifts as a result of these variables remains unknown, but this may possibly be determined empirically in future research. However, because of the nature of the demand curve, the extent of the shifts may be quite limited.

DISCUSSION

We have tried to show how suicidal behavior might be viewed by a demand and supply analysis. The demand curve for suicide appears to be an upward sloping curve, with the level of distress that is relieved by death as the equivalent of "price." The higher the individual's level of distress, the higher his probability of completing suicide. On the other hand, the supply curve is downward sloping, indicating that the higher the cost of completing suicide the less likely it is that the individual will kill himself.

If the probability of committing suicide is less than the equilibrium probability, the person will feel less distress and the cost of committing suicide becomes quite high. Thus, the person will be less likely to kill himself. On the other hand, if the probability of committing suicide is higher than the equilibrium, the person will feel a higher level of distress and the cost of committing suicide will be quite low. Thus he becomes more likely to kill himself.

However, careful examination of the important factors that might affect the demand and supply for suicide shows that many of these variables do not vary greatly from year to year. Thus, the demand curve probably does not shift too much as a result of small changes in these variables. An economic analysis, therefore, would focus on the supply side for the most effective means of changing the probability that a person will kill himself.

APPLYING THE MODEL:
THE EFFECT OF THE AVAILABILITY OF METHODS FOR SUICIDE

When a person is contemplating suicide, the availability of a method for suicide should contribute to the use of that method for suicide by that person. For the entire population as a whole, the availability of a method for suicide should be responsible for the changing rates of suicide in general (Clarke and Lester, 1989).

Let us take firearms as an example. In the last thirty years, the suicide rate in the United States has been increasing. During this period, the rate of suicide using firearms has also been increasing while the rate of suicide using other methods has been decreasing. As shown in Table 7.1, in 1959 the overall suicide rate was 10.5 per 100,000 people per year, the firearm suicide rate 4.7, and the non-firearm suicide rate 5.8. In 1984, the total suicide rate was 12.4, the firearm suicide rate 7.2, and the non-firearm suicide rate 5.1. The increase in the overall suicide rate by 1984 was due entirely to the increase in the firearm suicide rate. Interestingly enough, the same period also witnessed a very substantial increase in the number of guns in circulation (Boyd, 1983).

Another common method for suicide is motor vehicle exhaust, and the frequency of the use of car exhaust for suicide has changed in recent years. In the last few decades, the imposition of emission controls on cars in the United States led to a reduction in the amount of carbon monoxide in car exhaust, making suicide more difficult to carry out (since the exhaust was less poisonous) unless the emission system was disconnected (Clarke and Lester, 1987). The carbon monoxide content of General Motors cars declined from 8.5% in 1968 to 0.5% in 1980. Since car exhaust was less toxic, car exhaust has become less effective as a method for suicide, and so we expect that the suicide rate using car exhaust should have decreased since 1950. The present study attempts to test this causal relationship, that is, a lower toxicity of car exhaust should result in a lower rate of suicide using that method.

One problem with studying the impact of emission controls on suicide by means of car exhaust is that many multi-car families have older cars as well as newer cars. Also, people can affect the efficacy of the emission controls on newer cars by neglecting the servicing of their car and by using leaded gasoline.

One way of measuring the toxicity of car exhaust over time in the United States may be to use the accidental death rate from car exhaust. The more toxic car exhaust is in the nation, the higher the accidental death rate from car exhaust should be.

Applying the demand and supply model to car exhaust, if the toxicity of car exhaust is reduced, then car exhaust becomes more difficult to use as a method for suicide because its use necessitates mechanical knowledge and efforts to make it lethal. According to the model, suicide will become a less accessible act. Therefore, if other factors remain constant, we can predict a cause-and-effect relationship between the toxicity of car exhaust (measured in the present study by the accidental death rate from car exhaust) and the rate of its use for suicide. The higher the toxicity of car exhaust the greater the chance of success in attempts to commit suicide, thereby leading to a higher rate of suicide using car exhaust.

We obtained data on the number of suicides by motor vehicle exhaust, suicides by all other methods, and accidental deaths from motor vehicle exhaust from the annual volume of *Vital Statistics of the United States* published by the National Center for Health Statistics; data on the population of the United States from the *Statistical Abstract of the United States, 1987* published by the Bureau of the Census; and data on the number of cars per capita from the *Highway Statistics, Summary to 1985*, published by the Federal Highway Authority for the period of 1950 to 1984.

We ran regression analyses on three dependent variables: the percentage of suicides using motor vehicle exhaust, the suicide rate using car exhaust and the suicide rate by all other methods. The predictor variables were the accidental death rate from motor vehicle exhaust and the number of cars per capita. Since the number of cars per capita rose progressively each year from 1950 to 1984, this variable is similar to a simple time trend.

The results are shown in Table 7.2. It can be seen that, the higher the accidental death rate from car exhaust (implying a more toxic car exhaust), the greater the percentage of suicides using car exhaust and the higher the suicide rate from car exhaust.

Table 7.2. Results of the Multiple Regression

Predictor Variables

Dependent Variables	accidental death rate from car exhaust		cars/capita	
	regression coefficient		regression coefficient	
	b	p	b	p
percent of suicides using car exhaust	0.87	< .01	-0.44	= .03
suicide rate using car exhaust	1.04	< .01	0.15	ns
suicide rate by all other means	-0.01	ns	0.83	< .01

The accidental death rate using car exhaust was not related to the rate of completed suicide by all *other* methods. This can be seen in Table 7.2, where the calculated regression coefficient was not significantly different from zero, suggesting that those who might have used car exhaust for suicide did not switch to other methods for suicide as car exhaust became less toxic. (If people switched to other methods for suicide as car exhaust became less toxic, we would expect a significant negative regression coefficient.)

The time trend (cars per capita) indicates that the percentage of suicides using car exhaust decreased over the period and the suicide rate by means other than car exhaust increased over the period, while the suicide rate using car exhaust did not vary monotonically over the period.

The higher the accidental death rate (which implies a more toxic car exhaust), the greater the percentage of suicides using car exhaust and the higher the suicide rate from car exhaust. This major conclusion of the study confirms the prediction from the economic model namely that, as the cost of suicide increases, the rate of suicide decreases. The low toxicity of car exhaust calls for greater time and effort to make its use successful for suicide, involves a higher cost for suicide, and so leads to a lower rate of suicide using that method.

The implication of this empirical result is that, for any of the available methods for suicide, restricting the availability of the method will reduce the suicide rate. This suggests that the use of firearms for suicide might be lessened by making ownership less easy through licensing, waiting periods between purchase and delivery of the firearm, or by a total prohibition against the purchasing of certain types of firearms. Similarly, the prescription of drugs that are potentially lethal could be monitored by physicians more carefully and the drugs could be prescribed in smaller amounts.

References

Barnes, C. The partial effect of income of suicide is always negative. *American Journal of Sociology*, 1975, 80, 1454-1462.

Boyd, J. H. The increasing rate of suicide by firearms. *New England Journal of Medicine*, 1983, 308, 872-874.

Clarke, R. V. & Lester, D. Toxicity of car exhausts and opportunity for suicide. *Journal of Epidemiology and Community Health*, 1987, 41, 114-120.

Clarke, R. V., & Lester, D. *Suicide: closing the exits.* New York: Springer-Verlag, 1989.

Kitagawa, E., & Hauser, P. *Differential mortality in the United States.* Cambridge: Harvard University Press, 1973.

Lea, S. E. G. The psychology and economics of demand. *Psychological Bulletin,* 1987, 85, 441-466.

Lester, D. Sex differences in suicidal behavior. In E. Gomberg & V. Franks (Eds.) *Gender and disordered behavior.* New York: Brunner/Mazel, 1979, 287-300.

Lester, D. *Why people kill themselves.* Springfield: Charles Thomas, 1983.

Lester, D. *Suicide as a learned behavior.* Springfield: Charles Thomas, 1988.

Stack, S. Suicide. *Social Forces,* 1978, 57, 644-653.

Stack, S. Durkheim's theory of fatalistic suicide. *Journal of Social Psychology,* 1979, 107, 161-168.

CHAPTER 8

HAMERMESH AND SOSS'S
MICROECONOMIC THEORY OF SUICIDE

The economic theory of suicide developed by Hamermesh and Soss (1974) is based on a utility function which is determined by the permanent income and the current age of the individual. The permanent income is the average income expected over a person's lifetime. In the calculation of the permanent income, the authors followed a formula that includes the real income of the current year and the rest of the years of working life of an individual. Thus, this brings in a concept of opportunity cost, that is, by committing a suicide, an individual forgoes the opportunity of earning income in the rest of his or her life.

The permanent income and the current age of an individual determine the consumption level from which an individual will derive satisfaction. The current age also determines the cost of maintaining the day-to-day life of the individual, which is a negative attribute to the utility function.

A third element of the economic attributes to suicide is the taste for living or distaste for suicide, which is assumed to be a parameter normally distributed with a zero mean and constant variance. When the total discounted lifetime utility (which includes the taste for living) remaining to a person reaches zero, an individual will commit suicide.

This economic model of suicide contains the following assumptions. (1) The older the current age, the lower the total satisfaction, because the cost of day-to-day living increases with age. (2) The greater the permanent income, the higher the total satisfaction, since a higher income level warrants a higher consumption level. However, the additional satisfaction brought forth by additional income decreases with higher income.

Based on the principle of utility maximization in this economic model, we can derive several theorems about the suicide rate of a society. First, the suicide rate will increase with age. Since the marginal utility of lifetime income decreases with increased permanent income, the older an individual gets, the less additional satisfaction he is going to derive from consumption. This should increase the probability that the person will commit suicide.

Secondly, the suicide rate will be inversely related to permanent income. If an individual receives a greater amount of lifetime income, he is expected to have a greater amount of consumption and, therefore, a greater satisfaction from life. This should decrease the probability of committing suicide.

Crouch (1979) presented a model similar to that of Hamermesh and Soss. He began with the idea that an individual will commit suicide if the sum of his enjoyments from life (E) and his distaste for suicide (D) falls to or below zero, that is, when

$$E + D < 0$$

Enjoyment for life depends upon the full income of the individual and loved ones and their living expenses which are a function of the individual's age.

(1) As the full income of the individual and/or his loved ones increases, the probability of suicide decreases and vice versa.

(2) The higher the living expenses, the less the life enjoyment for the individual and so the greater the tendency to commit suicide.

(3) The more religious the individual is, the more distasteful his attitude toward suicide will be and so the less likely he will be to commit suicide. Crouch singled out the influence of Catholicism for his religious variable.

(4) Divorce (especially divorce that is opposed by the individual) and widowhood increase the likelihood of suicide because they decrease the full income of the family.

It can be seen that Crouch's formulation of suicidal behavior is based entirely on Hamermesh and Soss's idea of utility maximization. Crouch differs in defining income differently from Hamermesh and Soss (but fails to give a complete definition) and in including income from the individual's loved ones.

TESTS OF THE MODEL

Hamermesh and Soss examined the average male suicide rate by age in 21 developed countries for the years 1965 to 1967. In nine of these countries, the suicide rate rose monotonically with age; in two it peaked for the oldest age group but it did not rise steadily with age; and in eight countries it rose monotonically to peak in those aged 55 - 64. (The oldest age group in the analysis was 65 - 74 years old.) Only in two countries, Sweden and Poland, did the peak occur before this point, with the suicide rate dropping a little for the older age groups.

Lester (1982), in an analysis of age patterns of suicide in nations of the world, presented data that are relevant to Hamermesh and Soss's conclusion. Lester found an increasing suicide rate with age for males in thirteen nations, a peak in middle age for males in three nations, and a peak in old age with a minor peak in young adulthood for seven nations. For females, the numbers were six, seven, and five respectively. Thus, a monotonically increasing suicide rate with age is not the most common pattern.

Hamermesh and Soss also examined time series data for the male suicide rate in the United States for the years from 1947 to 1967. They incorporated the unemployment rate into the model, arguing that, when unemployment increases, people's expectations of future income (and utilities) are revised downward. Holding the real income of the employed constant, an increased number of people will believe future prospects to have diminished and will have a higher probability of committing suicide. Moreover, there is evidence that periods of unemployment last longer for older workers who are laid off and that older workers' expectations of finding new employment are affected by this phenomenon. Thus, unemployment is expected to have a positive association with suicide rates and an increasing effect on suicide in older workers.

Hamermesh and Soss tested the usefulness of their theory by using an econometric approach, an approach that places more weight on the efficient prediction of the target variable than on whether the form of the variables used makes sociological or psychological sense. The equation used was:

$$S(A,t) = a_0 + a_1I(A,t) + a_2I^2(A,t) + a_3A + a_4A^2 + a_5A^3$$
$$+ a_6UN(A,t) + a_7UN(a,t).A + v_{A,t}$$

where
   A is the age group
   t is the year
   I is the discounted permanent income of age group A at time t
   UN is the unemployment rate of age group A at time t
   a_i are constants

   v is a disturbance term

Note the presence of higher order powers in some of the terms. Rather than conducting separate time series analyses for each age group, Hamermesh and Soss pooled the data for the 21-year period and for the nine age groups, giving 189 pooled observations.

The empirical results presented by Hamermesh and Soss showed that permanent income was negatively related to the suicide rate while the unemployment rate had a positive association with the suicide rate and an increasing effect on suicide as workers become older as predicted. Yet as income has risen in the postwar period, the male suicide rate has fallen for most age groups. Only for the youngest three age groups (those aged 20-34 years) has the suicide rate risen with rising incomes, a result that is in contrast with the prediction of the theory. Hamermesh and Soss explained this by arguing that the expansion in the number of people pursuing education into their twenties and the consequent postponement of consumption by an increased fraction of the people in these groups could affect the prediction. The decline in suicide rates for older people as their income has increased may be especially strong because of the decrease in variability of income resulting from the expansion of Social Security benefits. Indeed, Hamermesh and Soss pointed out that there was a sharp drop in the relative suicide rates of groups over age 55 in the late 1930s coincident with the introduction of Social Security.

Hamermesh and Soss also analyzed suicide rates among the people in eight different occupations: professionals, managers, clericals, sales, craftsmen, operatives, service workers, and laborers. They found that the suicide rate was generally lower among the occupation groups in which income was greater in three cities for which they had data (Chicago, New Orleans, and Tulsa).

Finally, in a cross-sectional study of the suicide rate of white males in 38 states for which data on income by age and race were available, they added the variable of the percentage of Roman Catholic parochial school enrollments and a dummy variable for the three most western states (California, Oregon and Washington), removed the variables involving unemployment, and weighted each term with the proportion of white males in that age group in the state. They found a negative association between suicide rates and permanent income for all age groups except those aged 20-24.

Hamermesh (1974) applied the same time series model and research design to an analysis of the suicide rates of blacks for years from 1947 to 1967. The data showed, first, that the effect on the suicide rate of individual income was positive. This was contradictory to what was expected both from the theory and from the results from whites. Second, the effect of unemployment on the suicide rate was positive and increased with age. This was similar to the finding for whites. Third, for the prediction of the black suicide rate, Hamermesh included the white suicide rate as one of the independent variables, and the white suicide rate was found to play a part in predicting the black suicide rate.

Using cross-sectional data in both 1950 and 1960 from 20 states with large black populations, and using actual income rather than permanent income, a positive association between the suicide rate and income was observed. The association between suicide and unemployment was negative, and Hamermesh tried to explain away this anomalous result by attributing it to a decline in the statewide variation in black unemployment and to a similar decline in the variation in black unemployment by age.

Hamermesh offered two alternative explanations for the positive effect of income on suicide rate. Black suicide rates may have risen over the postwar period, not because of changes in relative incomes, but rather because blacks have become more aware of the economic conditions prevailing in the white population. Blacks whose incomes are higher are likely to be in closer contact with whites and are more aware of their income.

The second explanatory factor focused on possible differential under-reporting of suicides over time and across states. If under-reporting has decreased over time and is lower where incomes are higher, a positive bias will be generated to the estimates of the effect of income on the suicide rate.

DISCUSSION

Hamermesh and Soss have proposed a useful model for explaining the relationship of suicide rates to the economy. However, their tests of the model have involved the introduction of a number of arbitrary assumptions leading to the inclusion of terms in the regression equations that are hard to justify sociologically or psychologically. They made no effort to show whether the use of other assumptions would lead to validation or invalidation of the model.

Furthermore, while other investigators study either a sample of regions, a period of time, or a sample of groups in the society defined by particular socioeconomic variables, Hamermesh and Soss have frequently used a mixture of these categories, such as twenty-one years by nine age groups resulting in 189 observations, an unorthodox procedure. Added to this is their frequent use of *post hoc* explanations of discrepant results. Thus, their model cannot be judged to have been adequately tested and confirmed as yet.

REFERENCES

Crouch, R. *Human behavior*. North Scituate, MA: Duxbury, 1979.

Hamermesh, D. S. The economics of black suicide. *Southern Economic Journal*, 1974, 41, 188-199.

Hamermesh, D. S., & Soss, N. M. An economic theory of suicide. *Journal of Political Economy*, 1974, 82, 83-98.

Lester, D. The distribution of sex and age among completed suicide. *International Journal of Social Psychiatry*, 1982, 28, 256-260.

CHAPTER 9

IMPULSE-FILTERING AND REGRESSION MODELS OF THE DETERMINATION OF THE RATE OF SUICIDE[4]

ROGER A. McCAIN[5]

Econometric studies indicate that economic conditions are among the determinants of aggregate rates of suicide (see, for example, Yang [1989]). Modern economic theory generally models individual choices as the results of maximization of expected lifetime utility. These two points suggests a model of the decision for self-destruction along the lines of Hamermesh and Soss (1974; Hamermesh, 1974). In a model of this sort, the individual commits suicide when and if the discounted present value of expected future utility (contingent on continued life) becomes negative. However, this hypothesis conflicts with the strong, if unsystematic, casual impression that many suicides are not rational acts in any such sense; and in this context one thinks in particular of youth suicides.[6]

---

[4] This paper is dedicated to the memory of Alan Mills, who died by his own hand in 1962 at the age of nineteen.

[5] Professor of Economics, Drexel University, Philadelphia, PA 19104.

[6] By contrast, suicides of the ill and elderly plausibly may conform more nearly to the negative-future-utility model. On this, note Tolchin (1989). Tolchin observes, however, that perception of suicides by the elderly as rational may lead to an expectation that the old should destroy themselves. This would seem to be a cognitive fallacy -- what is rational is not mandatory! -- but cognitive fallacies may in fact affect behavior, if individuals are not maximizers of lifetime utility.

This chapter sketches an alternative theory of choice, which allows for a broader range of motives and for choices that are simply contrary to one's self-interest,[7] and relates it to the decision for self-destruction. The model offered rests on the interaction of a random stream of *impulses* with a set of motivational *filters*; thus it is a model of *impulse-filtering*. Maximization of expected future utility is subsumed as a special case, but will not in general be realized.[8] A summary of the impulse-filtering model is first given, and it is then related to antisocial and irrational behavior in general and to self-destructive behavior in particular.

A New Theory of Choice

Economists ordinarily think of choices as being choices of market baskets. However, we shall begin with choices among alternatives of a more elementary kind. The elementary choices are binary choices: shall I act in a certain way, yes or no? With this in view, I posit that human choice behavior arises from the interaction of a stream of *impulses* with a system of *filters*. The elementary choice then is the choice to act on a particular impulse, or not to act on it. Not to act on the impulse is to filter that impulse out of one's action. The impulses are at least in part random. The filtering process is the deterministic aspect of the choice process.

The role of impulses was suggested to me in part by Becker's (1962) paper on irrational behavior,[9] and in part by Schrodinger's (1967) proposal on the mind-body problem. It has been observed that brain cells sometimes

---

[7] McCain (1990) discusses the model as a theory of economic choice and also relates it to the philosophical literature on freedom of will.

[8] McCain (1991) explores a special case in which choices converge to utility maximization and contrasts some cases in which this convergence may fail.

[9] Becker offers two models of irrational behavior: one random and one purely inertial except insofar as changes of constraints force changes of choice. He then argues that the main propositions of comparative statics can be derived nevertheless. However, a model of simply irrational behavior is even less use than one of purely rational behavior. (Simply random choice from the entire choice set, or purely inertial behavior, is almost certainly counterempirical, although to the best of my knowledge the test has not been tried.) The impulse-filtering model is advanced as a model which allows for *more or less* thoroughly rational decisions, incorporating elements both of randomness and inertia.

"fire" (make the transition from the dormant to the excited state) with no apparent cause. Schrodinger suggested that the brain cells might be so sensitive that this spontaneous firing could be the result of inherently random events at the sub-atomic level. Moreover, such a spontaneous firing could then result in the excitation of a number of brain cells, and then a larger number, until the spontaneous firing cascades into a macroscopic action -- for example, to use the chestnut from the free-will literature, the person raises his or her arm. I would modify that only in saying that the person has an impulse to raise his or her arm.

The impulses are the main active, moving aspect of the impulse-filtering model. Some impulses may occur (as Schrodinger [1967] thought) because of the purely random quantum processes of the brain. Others may be determined within the brain, but derive their unpredictable character from chaotic or similar nonlinear dynamics. It is not necessary that all impulses be unpredictable, or that every aspect of the impulse-stream be random. Some impulses may be the predictable results of sense-stimuli, as the impulse to strike back when assaulted (or to kiss back when kissed). Some may be predictable consequences of physiological events. Importantly, the rate of occurrence of impulses may be affected by the subject's state of arousal. What the theory requires is that some, perhaps a small proportion, of impulses are unpredictable on the basis of a data set which excludes the internal history of the choosing subject.

Now, Schrodinger may have gone too far in attributing spontaneous nerve-cell excitation to quantum-physical indeterminacy, and that conjecture is not a part of the impulse-filtering theory. But it is one possibility, and it illustrates three important points about impulses. First, an impulse has two aspects: it is both a neurophysiological and a mental event. Thus, nerve cells become excited and reflect "perhaps I will raise my arm -- to reach for that cup of tea." Both descriptions are equally valid descriptions of the same event. Second, such an event may indeed result from quite small physical causes, such as spontaneous excitation of a single nerve cell. The modern developments in nonlinear mathematics (such as bifurcation theory, chaos theory, and catastrophe theory) provide models for such occurrences which were not available to Schrodinger. Third, therefore, our understanding of the impulses may well be increased by a highly reductionist program of research. But this program would be neuropsychological, not social-scientific, and in what follows the impulses will be considered only in their macroscopic and mental aspect ("I think I shall raise my arm").

The impulses are then supposed to pass through one or more "filters." The filters determine whether the impulse is acted upon, suppressed, or transformed. These filters are aspects of the person as a *whole* and some will change as the person grows, depending on the person's unique experience.

For example, in McCain (1991), I present an impulse-filtering model which encompasses standard "utility maximization" as a special and limiting case. In this model, the choices are indeed "market baskets," and the impulses are revisions of the previously consumed market basket. These revisions are distributed in a random way around the previous basket. The revision then is accepted (and made the basis for subsequent further revisions) if the revision yields a higher utility than the previous market basket, and is suppressed otherwise. If the utility function is stable and mathematically regular, this process converges to a maximum of utility, just as we might expect. (In other, more interesting cases, it does not.) The process is called "groping," for reasons which will probably be obvious, and the model based on it will be called the "groping" model.

But the groping model is oversimple, in that it leaves reason out of the picture. Now, one might have thought that a theory of "rational choice" would mean a theory of choice based on, or involving, reason. In fact, reason, by which I mean cognitive processes, plays no part in the choice theory of "neoclassical" economics, nor do cognitive processes play a large part in the groping model. Moreover, reason is the presumable basis for any choice of future over present benefits (time preference), of anticipated over concrete benefits (expectations, rational or not), and thus in any decision based on expected future lifetime utility. We may take it, then, that cognitive processes usually play some role in human decision-making. These cognitive processes are wide-ranging -- the practices of consulting cartomancers and econometricians, of calculating break-even charts and spreadsheets are included, as is flipping a coin -- but they undoubtedly often play a part in choice. Thus, we must posit at least one filter in addition to the incremental utility filter: the cognitive filter. This is the filter of reason, and we must look primarily to cognitive psychology for understanding of its function.

Now, the impulse-filtering model need not stand or fall with any one list of filters. Only the cognitive filter seems essential, and different subsidiary hypotheses might be proposed with respect to other filters in the decision-processes of the representative person. Indeed, it may be that individuals differ, some filtering in one way and others filtering in other ways, and these differences may or may not be pathological. Nevertheless, something more needs be said about filters other than the incremental-utility and cognitive filters.

One of these will be of particular concern for a theory of suicide. It is the filter of social conformity. Economists apart, most social scientists would agree that a great deal of human behavior is determined by socialization.[10] This view sees social norms as among the primary determinants of behavior, and has powerful empirical support. But a key point in favor of the impulse-filtering model is its capacity to allow for pluralism in the determinants of human behavior. Thus, socio-cultural elements, which are usually left out of economic research, offer at least as much promise in predicting economic behavior as do prices and incomes. One way to introduce these influences is to posit a filter of social conformity. The working of this filter will be expressed by the reflection, "People like me just don't do things like that." Social norms, learned in the process of acculturation, and the corresponding social reference groups, will then be a major part of the content of that filter; conversely, the filter of social conformity mediates the social norms.

In addition, there may be filters of emotion, fear, and neurosis. Clinical psychology has been concerned with the details of individual behavior in a way that has made it easy for economists to ignore. Neurosis, phobia, and similar phenomena may well be insignificant for the average tendencies of behavior with which economists are most often concerned. Supposing that individuals are neurotic and phobic, what does this tell us about the average person's demand for tomatoes and how to model it? Nevertheless, con-

---

[10] For a more powerful recent restatement of this kind, see Etzioni (1988).

cepts of neurosis and phobia challenge the rational-choice model in an obvious and provocative way, and will be important for a theory of suicide. I would tentatively posit a set of emotional filters, which would include such things as phobias and obsessive behaviors. The importance of such filters in actual individual behavior would seem likely to vary from person to person and according to states of arousal and mood.

One further point about the impulse-filtering model may be important for a theory of suicide. With multiple filters, indecision is a possibility. It is possible that no impulse can pass all of the filters. In such a case, the individual may be in some sense immobilized.[11] This immobility, in itself, is not indecision. However, it may also be that the continuation of the existing situation is infeasible. Then the individual can neither change nor continue, and is simply indecisive.

THE COGNITIVE FILTER AND WEAKNESS OF WILL

In the light of the impulse-filtering model, the cognitive filter is not simply one among the several filters. It differs from the other filters in several important ways. First, it can transform the action of the other filters. Perhaps it is in this way that indecision is overcome: the individual realizes that the decision between the filters must be made, and chooses one -- suppressing the other filter so that impulses consistent with the other filter, but not with the one suppressed, are nevertheless acted upon. Similarly, in making intertemporal choices, the act of imagination which conceives of future satisfactions as substitutes for present satisfaction is an act of cognition which transforms another filter (a filter of incremental utility, if such is possible, or of basic needs or esthetic satisfactions, etc.) by translating its satisfaction from present to future time.

Second, the cognitive filter is constantly changing. In this sense, the cognitive filter is a second major active element in economic (indeed in

---

[11] This immobility need not be literal. The filters that determine the individual's day-to-day routines may allow for some flexibility of response -- but no *change of routine* is possible, since any change of routine will be blocked by one filter or another.

human) action, along with (but ultimately driven by) the stream of impulses. Indeed, every act which is remembered (and every impulse the suppression of which is remembered) changes the cognitive system. For that system includes the memory, and memory plays a part in every cognitive act, including filtering. The obvious economic example is the memory of a good or bad experience with a branded good which leads us to suppress or act upon the impulse to purchase it again, as the case may be.

Third, there also seems to be a strong tendency for the cognitive inventory to be reorganized along lines which are more "consistent." This is the implication of work on cognitive dissonance (Festinger, 1957), the significance of which for economics has been indicated by Akerlof and Dickens (1982). (It should be kept in mind, however, that the principle by which consistency is judged is not objective and external, but is a self-referential part of the cognitive inventory itself and so subject to its own reorganization). This will interact with the filters of social conformity, as we shall see.

As an illustration of the application of the role of the cognitive filter in impulse-filtering theory, consider the problem of weakness of will. "Weakness of will" is a key concept in the philosophical literature on will and has played some part in some recent economic writing (Thaler and Shefrin, 1981; Schelling, 1980; Elster, 1977). A common example of "weakness of will" is due to Schelling, who tells us that he has placed his alarm clock on his bureau, across the room from his bed. The idea is that he cannot turn it off without getting up and walking across the room -- and that by that time, he is awake enough so that he does not turn the clock off and go back to sleep. Thus, he traps his weak-willed, sleepy self into awakening. Weakness of will is very difficult to reconcile with a model in which choices are determined by stable preferences and objective constraints, as economic theory generally assumes; and Elster and Schelling have assumed the existence of at least two utility functions, of which one corresponds to the individual's will, in some authentic sense, but the other is sometimes decisive in particular decisions.

In the context of impulse-filtering, the key point is that some of the filters may be active to different degrees under different circumstances. The state of arousal may be an important determinant of the relative activity of filters. This is particularly true of the cognitive filter, which, for example, is largely if not entirely inactive in sleep and may be relatively ineffective in such other circumstances as drunkenness. In these circumstances impulses may be passed which would in other circumstances be filtered. In the common phrase, such behavior is "impulsive" (Black, 1991). Such behavior includes instances of "weakness of will."

The same example will serve to illustrate how some choices may be "irrational." Will quite aside, when I set my alarm clock I may have a rationale for doing so -- for example, that I feel better when I keep a regular schedule of sleeping or waking, or that my boss will fire me if I am late, or that I will maximize my lifetime utility by getting up early on this particular date. Thus, to get up is rational (in the sense that not to do so goes against a rationale to which I am committed). A rationale is a cognitive phenomenon, though. When the cognitive filter is inactive, because of drowsiness, I may not filter impulses which go against the rationale. In particular (of course) I may not filter the impulse to turn off that darned alarm clock. In failing to do so, I act irrationally.

SOCIAL NORMS, EMULATION, AND DESTRUCTIVE BEHAVIOR

Destructive and antisocial behavior presents difficulties for economic theory, and, indeed, even for the broader theories proposed by some of the critics of neoclassical economics. The difficulty is that it is not at all clear that these acts are in anyone's interest. Even in the bi-utility theory proposed by Etzioni (1988) and Lutz and Lux (1988), the problem is not resolved. In these models, the individual has two preference systems or utility functions: one which is self-interested and the other which reflects moral or ethical values. In such a case, the worst that the individual can do is act selfishly. The impulse-filtering model includes the possibility that individuals may be worse than that.[12] The key point is that all sorts of impulses occur with some positive (however small) probability. They then

---

[12] In Etzioni's terms, the model is consistent with (though it does not require) an "oversocialized Tory" view of human nature.

may or may not be filtered. In explaining the occurrence of antisocial acts, we are explaining the circumstances in which these impulses are not filtered but instead expressed.

Consider fads of violent or destructive acts. Fads are a familiar feature of life. Young males may choose, in one period, to comb long hair back into greasy duck-tails, and in another, to dye their hair pink on one side and shave it on the other. Older people may feel, in one period, that it is important that their car be American made, and in another period, that it ought to be Swedish. But these imitative phenomena have a darker side. For a time, the poisoning of pain-killers capsules may become a commonplace in the news. Reports of shootings at cars on the freeway and of youth suicides have sometimes also become common. Now, neoclassical economics might be able to rationalize the first group of events, by positing something like an utility-of-conformity; but it would seem to be very unlikely that freeway shooters are maximizing anything, however great their taste for violence might be. But we can give an account of these events in terms of impulse-filtering.

Let us consider the highway shootings. I suspect that the impulse to shoot another driver has been a pretty common one since cars became common possessions, and I can testify that I have felt it from time to time. Nevertheless, this impulse has been suppressed almost always. The filters which suppressed it may have been ethical or cognitive (the fear of apprehension and punishment would be the latter), but in at least some cases, the active filter was the filter of conformity -- "real people just don't do that."

However, at a particular time and place, one individual gives vent to the impulse and takes a shot. This event is not a predictable one. Perhaps the person is sociopathic (has no effective filters of any kind against antisocial behavior), or perhaps he simply chooses evil. In any case, the act is publicized in some detail. Among other persons for whom the social conformity filter is the effective filter, there is new sensory evidence inconsistent with the rule that "people like me don't do that." Cognitive dissonance thus, in some cases, leads to reorganizations of the cognitive inventory, which reduce the effectiveness of the social conformity filter against violence. Thus an "epidemic" of imitative shootings occurs. It should be noted that the proportion of the population affected is very small -- statistically insignificant, without doubt -- but the impact on people's feeling of security on the highways may well not have been insignificant, statistically or otherwise.

A personal note may highlight the point. It has been widely reported that the epidemic of violence like the above began in, and was largely limited to, southern California. In fact, however, several similar events had occurred in Shreveport, Louisiana, prior to the reported Los Angeles events. These were reported on local Shreveport television (I observed them while visiting relatives there) but not nationally. The tendency of these events to correspond to the local news coverage is strong, if casual, evidence of their imitative character. This may set the stage for the next section, which will deal with the extreme of self-destructive violent behavior: suicide.

Self-Destruction

Reference has been made to the economic theory of suicide developed by Hamermesh and Soss (1974). This economic theory of suicide is consistent with some empirical evidence. But the evidence is inherently inconclusive. Consistent with much econometric practice, it is comprised of rejections of the null hypothesis that price and income variables do not influence the rate of suicide. This does not bear at all on the question whether other variables, inconsistent with a lifetime-utility maximizing theory of suicides, may also affect suicide rates. Epidemics of imitative suicides would provide an example. It is not asserted here that such epidemics do occur: we shall treat the hypothesis of their occurrence as an example for contrasting two theories. The hypothesis might be tested (for example) by estimating models of suicide rates which include epidemological as well as economic determinants of suicide rates, thus embedding the economic hypothesis in a broader one.

For an impulse-filtering theory of suicides, we may begin with the impulses. On the assumption that impulses are at least partly random, we would expect that impulses to self-destruction would always occur with some measurable probability. Presumably, they are usually filtered. An incremental-utility filter certainly could be an important one in this process. It is quite plausible that a person might say to himself -- either consciously or unconsciously -- "I shall not destroy myself, because life is good." And this may mean simply that life is good *now*; it may express a passing mood. But economic theory is based on an assessment of lifetime *utility*, and the assessment of lifetime utility requires the intervention of the cognitive filter. This in turn introduces the possibility that the filter of lifetime utility may fail, due to biased cognitive processing. The likelihood of such failure would be dependent also on states of arousal and emotion.[13]

Nevertheless, the impulse-filtering model does predict that economic conditions will affect suicide rates. All that this requires is that the filtering is likelier (and thus suicide less likely) when "lifetime utility" is higher, even if the base rate of suicide is determined by other and "noneconomic" considerations. This prediction applies even if the decisions are biased away from rationality (for example, through excessive optimism or pessimism, or an exaggerated tendency to view the future as like the present). Even if the decisions are biased away from rationality, the direction of response -- less suicide when there is more lifetime income -- would be preserved, provided that the bias itself is roughly constant.

Here again, as with other forms of destructive behavior, we should not overlook the role of a filter of simple conformity in determining decisions for or against self-destruction. "I shall not destroy myself because 'real people' don't do that." Suppose that the usual filter against suicide is the filter of lifetime utility (or something functionally like it), but recall also that the lifetime-utility filter, requiring as it does cognitive intervention, and dependent as it is on states of arousal and mood, may fail. Then there will be a certain proportion of cases in which the filter of conformity is the decisive filter. Should the person then learn that another, with whom he or she identifies, has committed suicide, this (through the cognitive consistency tendency) would in some cases reduce the effectiveness of the filter

---

[13] One common cognitive failure is a tendency to project the future as being like the present, to a greater degree than the objective evidence warrants, so that passing moods might be more important as determinants of decisions than a lifetime utility maximization hypothesis would forecast. Formally, this is a failure of the law of iterated expectations, as in Camerer, Lowenstein and Weber (1989).

of conformity in filtering impulses to suicide. This leads to a prediction that "epidemics" of suicides might be observed; that is, that suicide would be more likely when the individual knows of a role model who has committed suicide. It should be stressed that we are discussing rare events, which may be more or less rare depending on circumstances, but which remain absolutely rare, and thus the appropriate protocols would be those for the study of a rare but hypothetically communicable disease.

It may be that some similar prediction could be coaxed out of the lifetime-utility model by positing some utility-of-conformity as an aspect of the utility-maximizing choice. Perhaps, however, this possibility may be dismissed as adding epicycles -- if indeed it is even logically possible.

The content of conformity may be conformity to internalized social norms, that is, moral prohibitions. The impulse-filtering model would also predict that moral prohibition would be an important determinant of self-destructive behavior. A moral filter may stop the impulse to suicide even when the lifetime-utility filter fails, and since the moral position is rather simple -- "thou shalt not" -- it requires little cognitive processing and so may be less sensitive to biased cognitive processing than is the lifetime utility filter. This leads to a prediction that ethnic groups with relatively strong religious traditions repressing suicide will have lower rates of suicide.[14] The lifetime-utility maximization hypothesis might support a similar prediction, if the moral norm based on socialization were to be incorporated in the utility function; but this sort of utility-maximization is not a straightforward extension of the more familiar theory. The utility loss from violating the prohibition would presumably have to be treated as a lump-sum cost. The detailed econometric implications of such a theory do not seem to have been clarified. Rather, the straightforward and prima facie interpretation of ethnicity as a determinant of suicide would clearly be that this behavior reflects socialization, and the impulse-filtering model provides a model for the integration of economic (lifetime utility) and socialization determinants.

---

[14] Yang's (1989) result, in a time-series study of the U.S., was contrary to this. However, her study did not allow for urbanization, and this may have been a confounding variable.

DISCUSSION

The conclusion of this section, then, is that suicide may be affected by economic variables and still not be (in most cases) "rational." Rather it may be (in most cases) a result of failures of the cognitive filter, through biased thinking or through simple inactivity of the cognitive filter, or a combination of both. The existence of some "rational suicides" is not excluded, but this would be a case in which the base rate of suicides would be determined by nonrational processes, while economic variables would determine deviations from the base rate. The impulse-filtering theory would share the predictions of the economic theory of suicide, so far as the economic variables are concerned, but would have other implications that the economic theory does not share. It is beyond the scope of this chapter to consider the empirical evidence that might decide the matter.

REFERENCES

Akerlof, G., & Dickens, W. T. The economic consequences of cognitive dissonance. *American Economic Review*, 1982, 72, 307-319.

Becker, G. S. Irrational behavior and economic theory. *Journal of Political Economy*, 1962, 70, 1-13.

Black, R. Endogenous demand for alcohol and self-command: a model of the temperance solution. In R. Franz, H. Singh, & J. Gerber (Eds.) *Handbook of Behavioral Economics*. Greenwich, CT: JAI Press, 453-469.

Camerer, C., Lowenstein, G., & Weber, M. The curse of knowledge in economic settings: an experimental analysis. *Journal of Political Economy*, 1989, 97, 1232-1254.

Elster, J. Ulysses and the Sirens: a theory of imperfect rationality. *Social Science Information*, 1977, 16, 469-526.

Etzioni, A. *The moral dimension.* New York: Free Press, 1988.

Festinger, L. *A theory of cognitive dissonance.* Palo Alto, CA: Stanford University Press.

Hamermesh, D. S., & Soss, N. M. Economic theory of suicide. *Journal of Political Economy,* 1974, 82, 83-98.

Hamermesh, D. S. Economics of black suicide. *Southern Economic Journal,* 1974, 41, 188-199.

Lutz, M., & Lux, K. *Humanistic economics: the new challenge.* New York: Bootstrap Press, 1988.

McCain, R. A. Impulse-filtering: a new model of freely willed economic choice. *Review of Social Economy,* 1990, 48, 125-171.

McCain, R. A. Groping: toward a behavioral metatheory of choice. In R. Franz, H. Singh, & J. Gerber (Eds). *Handbook of Behavioral Economics.* Greenwich, CT: JAI Press, 1991, 495-508.

Schelling, T. C. The intimate contest for self-command. *The Public Interest,* 1980, #60, 94-118.

Schrodinger, E. *What is life and man and matter?* New York: Cambridge University Press, 1967.

Thaler, R. H. & Shefrin, H. M. An economic theory of self-control. *Journal of Political Economy,* 1981, 89, 392-406.

Tolchin, M. When life is too much: suicide rises among the elderly. *The New York Times,* 1989, July 19, 1, 15.

Yang, B. Suicide and the economy. Conference of Atlantic Economic Society, Montreal, Canada, 1989.

CHAPTER 10

A "LIFE FORCE" PARTICIPATION PERSPECTIVE OF SUICIDE

WEI-CHIAO HUANG[15]

Suicide research transcends many disciplinary boundaries. While there exists voluminous literature on suicide in psychology, psychiatry, sociology and anthropology, economic analyses of suicide are very limited.[16] My objective here is to collaborate with the authors of this book in their efforts to present economic perspectives on suicide. As a labor economist, I will draw from the economic models of labor supply to conceptualize suicidal behavior. Specifically, the theoretical framework that has been used by economists to analyze an individual's decision to participate in the labor force will be adapted to understand how and why an individual decides to (or not to) participate in the "life market."

The economic theory of labor market participation is reviewed in the next section. Then, a "life market" participation perspective of suicide, which is analogous to the labor market participation framework, is presented and its implications discussed. A short conclusion follows in the last section.

---

[15] Assistant Professor of Economics, Western Michigan University, Kalamazoo, MI 49008-3899. The assistance and comments of my colleague, Professor Emily Hoffman, are greatly appreciated.
[16] Hamermesh and Soss (1974), Yeh and Lester (1987), and Yang (1989, 1990) are perhaps the only economic analyses which can be found.

ECONOMIC THEORY OF LIFE FORCE PARTICIPATION

Standard economic theory postulates that the individual attempts to maximize satisfaction or utility, which is derived from having income to purchase commodities and services and from enjoying leisure. The individual gains income from two sources: from supplying labor to the labor market and earning wages; and from receiving allowances or endowments from others, transfer payments from the government, and returns from accumulated assets and wealth. The former is usually called labor income and the latter nonlabor income. Given the limitation of time available in any period, a trade-off exists between getting more leisure and getting more labor income, both of which contribute to utility. Thus, in order to maximize utility, the individual has to choose an optimal combination of income and leisure (and hence the remaining time available for labor supply), subject to both the budget and time constraints.

There are broadly two solutions to this utility maximization problem: to participate in the labor market and forgo some amount of leisure, or not to participate in (or drop out of) the labor market. These solutions can be characterized graphically. In Figure 10.1, let U represent the extent of satisfaction, which is a function of Y, the level of income, and R, the amount of leisure. Y is determined by the sum of YO, the amount of nonlabor income, and YL, the labor income. YL is the product of W, the wage rate offered or available to the individual, and L, the amount of labor supply. By definition, R plus L equals T, the total time available. The individual's preferences for income and leisure are represented by the indifference curves, each of them showing the various combinations of income and leisure yielding an identical level of utility. You are equally well off anywhere on an indifference curve. The constraints facing the individual are shown as TEA and TEB for solutions A and B, respectively. The location and height of TE corresponds to the maximum possible amount of R (=T) and nonlabor income YO. The slopes of EA and EB are determined by the wage rates WA and WB, respectively. Obviously, WA > WB.

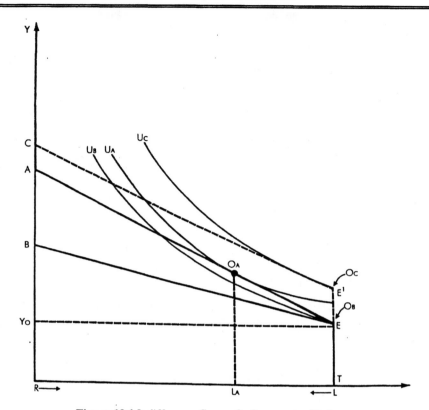

Figure 10.1 Indifference Curves for Incomes and Leisure

Solution A is depicted by the optimum OA, where the individual's highest attainable indifference curve, UA, is tangent to the budget line TEA. Thus, if the individual expects to receive WA from participating in the labor market, he will choose to work LA hours. On the other hand, if the expected wage from labor force participation is only WB and the budget line becomes TEB, no tangency or interior solution can be found. Instead, the solution (B) is depicted by the optimum OB, where the highest attainable indifference curve, UB, touches E, the corner of the budget constraint. In this case, the individual decides that it is best to enjoy the maximum leisure and to stay out of or to withdraw from the labor market.

Since the corner solution has important bearing on the choice of suicide to be discussed shortly, let us take a closer look at it. At OB, it is apparent that UB is steeper than EB, that is, the slope of UB at OB is greater than that of EB. As mentioned earlier, the slope of EB (in absolute value) is WB, whereas the slope of UB at OB indicates the amount of wage required to induce the individual to supply one unit of labor and maintain the same level of happiness. The latter is the minimum acceptable wage for labor force participation or, in short, the reservation wage. Thus, the individual chooses nonparticipation under the circumstance when the expected market wage is less than his reservation wage. This would occur when the individual experiences a wage cut and/or an increase in reservation wage. The former case can be shown in Figure 10.1: when wage drops from WA to WB the utility maximum changes from OA to OB. The latter could be caused by a change in tastes, which could be shown graphically by redrawing a whole set of more steeply sloped indifference curves in Figure 10.1.[17] However, being reluctant to cast away the sacred assumption of stable preferences, economists usually attribute the increase in reservation wage to the increase in nonlabor income with the assumption that leisure is a normal good. This can be shown by raising TE to TE' in Figure 10.1. As a result, the budget line shifts upward parallel to E'C, and the highest attainable indifference curve is now UC with the optimum at OC. Thus, due to the increase in nonlabor income, the reservation wage goes up making WA unattractive and motivating the individual to exit from the labor market.

Having delineated the basics of the labor force participation theory, we can now adapt them to analyze individual's "life force" participation decisions.

A "LIFE MARKET" PARTICIPATION PERSPECTIVE OF SUICIDE

In deciding whether or not to "participate" in living, the individual, as in the preceding section, is postulated to maximize utility (U) subject to constraints. In the context of life participation, the utility generating

---

[17] The redrawing of the indifference map is not shown in the figure so as to lessen the complexity of the diagram.

"income" (Y) needs to be interpreted more broadly. It encompasses all dimensions of the worth or value of life, anything that the individual cherishes and draws satisfaction from, such as love, health, fame, wealth, power, beauty, youth, eroticism, fun, adventure, prestige, respect, and security. Most of all these sorts of life income, however, need to be earned and maintained. One has to exercise and forgo some other enjoyments to achieve good health and strength,[18] to court and suffer to gain love, to endure and conceal anger to keep peace and harmony, to take tremendous pressure, anxiety, stress and to work extremely hard for financial and/or professional successes, etc. In short, "life is tough." Thus, life itself is a struggle; to live out a rewarding life requires a lot of hard "labor" (L) and efforts.

Of course, some of the life income is "nonlabor income" (YO), like the parental love, endowed fortune, God-blessed talents and health, and accumulated "wealth" and "assets." Even so, some of the nonlabor income such as assets are really hard-earned labor income (YL) accumulated from the past; they are regarded as nonlabor income in the current decision period. The opposite of work is "leisure" (R), which is, literally, rest, relax, or relief. Contrary to L, which entails living or work (such as facing up to difficulties), R is to let go of burdens, pressure, and responsibility, to give up on coping with problems, and to escape from pain, suffering, and the frustration of life by "living less" or taking it easy in living. Ultimately, the maximum manifestation of R is complete and permanent rest, that is, death. In a sense, L measures the extent of effort, enthusiasm, and resolve to live, and R measures its lack. Finally, W, the expected market wage rate, can be viewed as the perceived opportunity or ability to earn life income for a unit of life effort, that is, what living can pay or what life has to offer if one takes up living.

Again, two solutions are possible. For the vast majority of people, their optimum will be an interior solution like OA; they choose to live with varying amounts of effort and enthusiasm. Unfortunately for some, no in-

---

[18] The enjoyments of alcohol, drugs, sexual deviation and some other things can also be viewed as income as they generate utility for the individual, although they will conflict and offset the income of health, morality and other things. This model is meant to be flexible enough to accommodate even non-complementary incomes.

terior solutions can be found. As a consequence, they choose what seems to be the best solution for them, to drop out of the life market, that is to say, commit suicide. This act is conceptually analogous to discouraged workers dropping out of the labor market. There is, however, a notable difference between a termination of labor market participation and that of life market participation. Clearly, the discouraged worker may reassess the labor market in the next period and reenter if he so wishes, whereas death constitutes an absolutely irreversible biological cessation of life and therefore the suicide loses the option once for all to reenter the life market.

What leads to the decision to take one's own life? The framework presented here views suicide as resulting from the perceived obtainable wage in the life market falling short of one's minimum acceptable wage to live and thus making life not worth living. What makes one conclude that life is not worth living? Other things being equal, it is most likely caused by a sharp reduction of the perceived obtainable wage of living. The reduction of the expected wage from living is usually precipitated by a number of extreme life events: the confirmation of terminal disease, chronic illness, or recurring depressions, the loss or separation of significant others, the rejection of love, the fiasco of business, career, marriage, or grades, an impending defeat, disgrace, shame, or public humiliation, etc. All these make the individual want to simply "run away and hide" from the unbearable pain. Even if one does not want to give up and escape right away, the feeling of despair, hopelessness, and powerlessness created by those situations can make one cast enough doubt on one's ability and chance of coming out of the struggle, and still decide it is best to retreat from the battle. This view, interestingly, corresponds quite closely to Maris's (1981) definition that "suicide is self-killing deriving from one's inability or refusal to accept the terms of the human condition" (p. 290).

Although less likely, the decision to terminate life participation can also be caused by an increase in the reservation wage even when the market wage does not drop. One way to see this is to attribute this rise of the minimum acceptable wage to the increase in nonlabor income, which, for the most part, is the accumulated income earned in past periods. For a wealthy (in the sense of life) individual, he may need more stimuli to keep life interesting and challenging to live. Having so much of everything (fame, money etc.), and maybe too much, his utility from life wealth diminishes. He may become tired or bored of life, and he needs further excitement or "another mountain to conquer" to keep him going. Given a much higher reservation wage than ordinary people (or a much higher aspiration level, as in psychology), but without a matched increase in perceived wage (or ability), the individual may also find the corner solution to be more desirable and close the curtain of his life show on a high note.

Two implications follow from this life participation perspective of suicide which are worth noting. First, suicide, at least as portrayed here, is not irrational. The individual is assumed to engage in calculations of the benefits and costs of life market participation, and consciously and seriously to consider all available options, realizing the meaning and the irreversibility of death. It is only when one has exhausted other options and the corner solution appears to be the most desirable (or the least undesirable) choice that suicide takes place. Second, although committing suicide may be a calculated and rational act, it is not always correct. The future holds so many uncertainties and the life market information is always incomplete and imperfect. Considering that the W in our model is the perceived expected wage from living, it is very likely that the individual may be misinformed, may misinterpret the information, and may be mistaken in his calculation of life's worth. Granted that the individual may also incorporate the tremendous risk of erroneous assessment into his decision-making, it is conceivable that those life incidents mentioned earlier may be so enormously harsh as to distort his perception of being overwhelmingly negative.[19] Seeing no other viable options results in a miscalculated move, a real tragedy. This has obvious implications for suicide prevention. Some suicides are preventable if during the decision-making process the depressed or disturbed individual has external counseling to communicate the information and options more objectively, to show "the silver lining," and to enlarge the horizon and avoid oversights. Identifying potential sui-

---

[19] As stated elegantly by Brandt (1975): "Depression, like any severe emotional experience, tends to primitivize one's intellectual processes. It restricts the range of one's survey of the possibilities....But his best alternative is precisely a possibility he may overlook if, in a depressed mood, he thinks only of how badly off he is and cannot imagine any way of improving his situation."

cides or high risk persons to help is a task that can be taken up more skill-fully by psychiatrists and psychologists.

CONCLUSIONS

What causes a person to choose death over life? The objective of this chapter has been to conceptualize the individual's life/death decisions us-ing the theoretical approach from the economics of labor force participa-tion. Just as the labor force participant attempts to maximize utility by choosing an optimal amount of work, the life market participant also at-tempts to maximize the utility of life by "working in the life market" to earn "incomes." Also analogous to the situation in which a discouraged worker may decide to drop out of the labor market, a depressed individual may opt for exit from the life market and commit suicide. This occurs when the perceived market wage is less than the reservation wage, either because the precipitating harsh life incidents lower tremendously the per-ceived possible gains from living or because the minimum acceptable wage (the aspiration level) rises to an unachievable extent relative to the perceived wage or ability. This approach to suicidal behavior implies that suicide is rational and preventable.

REFERENCES

Brandt, R. B. The morality and rationality of suicide. In S. Perlin (Ed.) *A handbook for the study of suicide*. New York: Oxford University Press, 1975, 61-76.

Ehrenberg, R. G., & Smith, R. S. *Modern labor economics*. 3rd. Edition. Glenview, IL: Scott, Foresman, 1988.

Hamermesh, A. S., & Soss, N. M. An economic theory of suicide. *Journal of Political Economy*, 1974, 82, 83-98.

Maris, R. *Pathways to suicide*. Baltimore: John Hopkins University Press, 1981.

Yang, B. A real income hypothesis of suicide: A cross-sectional study of the United States in 1980. Eastern Economic Association, Annual Meeting, 1989.

Yang, B. The impact of the economy on suicide in different social and demographic groups: The U.S. experience. Eastern Economic Association, Annual Meeting, 1990.

Yeh, B. Y., & Lester, D. An economic model for suicide. In D. Lester (Ed.) *Suicide as a learned behavior.* Springfield, IL: Charles Thomas, 1987, 51-57.

CHAPTER 11

OTHER ECONOMIC MODELS OF SUICIDE

In most economic models for suicide, committing suicide is considered to be a rational act. An individual is acting "rationally" if, given a choice between various alternatives, he or she selected what seems to be the most desirable or least undesirable alternative. Thus, from this perspective, suicide can be a rational act. Economists are not concerned with whether suicide is wrong, immoral or a deviant act.

The economic models described in the previous chapters all fit into this definition of rationality perfectly, and there are other models postulated to show the rationality or irrationality of the suicidal behavior. The models proposed by Rosenthal (1993) and Dixit and Pindyck (1994) are presented in this chapter.

In addition, Becker's (1962) notion of rationality is examined here, together with Lester and Yang's (1991) application of the notion to suicidal behavior. Finally, psychological discussions of rationality by Wilber (1987) and Burns (1980) are applied to suicidal behavior.

SUICIDE ATTEMPTS AND SIGNALING GAMES

Rosenthal (1993) focused on suicide attempts which have chances of either success or failure, that is, suicide attempts of moderate to severe severity, where the individual is "gambling" with the outcome. He suggested that the suicide attempt can be seen as a signal intended to manipulate the receiver's behavior in a way favorable to the sender. As such, it resembles a game.

In this perspective, the sender may be either depressed or normal, and it is assumed that the players know the respective probabilities of these two possibilities. The sender knows his type while the receiver does not. The sender chooses an attempt (signal) strength (which determines whether he or she survives). The receiver then chooses a sympathetic or unsympathetic response. The receiver would prefer to respond sympathetically to a depressed sender and unsympathetically to a normal sender. Both types of sender would prefer a sympathetic response, but the preference is stronger in the depressed sender.

Rosenthal then examined Nash-equilibrium solutions, with the Cho-Kreps refinement and the Grossman-Perry refinement. His analysis suggested two hypotheses. First, gambling-type suicidal behavior would be less common if the suicidal individual strongly demanded a sympathetic response. Second, if the receiver is very likely to give a sympathetic response, then depressed senders are less likely to engage in gambling-type suicidal behavior.

SUICIDE AS INVESTMENT UNDER UNCERTAINTY

Dixit and Pindyck (1994) examined the nature of investment under conditions of uncertainty. Although their book focused on the investment decisions of firms, they noted that other decisions are made with the same conditions as investments: the decision is irreversible, there is uncertainty over the future rewards of the decision, and there is some leeway over the timing of the decision. Dixit and Pindyck noted that suicide fits these criteria. They noted that Hamermesh and Soss (1974) had argued that an individual will commit suicide when the expected value of the utility of the rest of his or her life falls short of some benchmark (or down to zero).

Dixit and Pindyck argued that Hamermesh and Soss failed to consider the option of staying alive. Suicide is irreversible, and the future is quite uncertain. Therefore, the option of waiting to see if the situation improves should be a likely choice. Even if the expected direction of life is downward, there may still be some non-zero positive probability that it will improve. Dixit and Pindyck speculated that suicides project the bleak present into an equally bleak future. They ignore the uncertainty of the future and the option value of life. In this respect, Dixit and Pindyck saw suicides as irrational.

They noted that religious and moral proscriptions against suicide compensate to some extent for this failure of rationality. These proscriptions raise the perceived cost of suicide and lower the threshold of the quality of life that precipitates suicide.

ECONOMIC DEFINITIONS OF IRRATIONALITY

Economists define rational behavior as maximizing some variable such as utility or profit. Becker (1962) defined two types of irrational behavior: (1) random, erratic and whimsical choices and (2) perseverative choices in which the person chooses what he or she has always chosen in the past. Lester and Yang (1991) argued that these two types of irrational behavior paralleled the major typology of suicidal behavior in which suicidal behavior is seen as a time-limited impulsive crisis or as a chronic maladaptive pattern.

Becker and Murphy (1988) have recently proposed a rational model for addictive behaviors in which they view addicts as rational optimizers, exhibiting consistent, forward-looking and individually optimal behavior. They have accurate perceptions of the trade-off between present benefits and future costs, and they are capable of making rational decisions based on these perceptions. A model for suicide might be based on such principles.

More recently, Fehr and Zych (1994) have proposed a theory of addictive behavior which they have called "irrationally myopic," in which people are assumed to base their decisions on the benefits which accrue immediately rather than on the costs which accrue over a longer period of time. This model may also be applicable to suicidal behavior.

IRRATIONALITY OR ARE THE PREMISES TRUE?

Wilber (1987) argued that suicides interpret their experiences differently from nonsuicidal people. They fail to realize that there are several options upon to them and, as a result, see suicide as the only way to deal with their intolerable circumstances. Their hopelessness makes their evaluation of their circumstances astigmatic. But, given their astigmatic perception of reality, their decision to commit suicide appears to be a logically valid deduction. Wilber is suggesting, therefore, that the premises of the suicidal person are false, but that their argument (or logic) is valid.

This issue is dealt with in detail by cognitive therapists who view the thinking patterns of all distressed people as irrational. Irrational thinking about events leads to pathological emotions and behavior, whereas rational thinking about events leads to appropriate emotions and behavior.

These ideas were originally formulated by Ellis (1973) in his rational-emotive therapy. Ellis described several common irrational thoughts that often underlie irrational thinking, such as the idea that we should be thoroughly competent, adequate and achieving in all possible respects in order to consider ourselves worthwhile, and the idea that certain people are bad, wicked and villainous and that they should be severely punished and blamed for their villainy.

Burns (1980) has described more general irrational thinking patterns such as overgeneralizing (in which one negative event is seen as part of a never-ending pattern of negative events) and catastrophizing (seeing a negative event as the worst thing that could ever happen to you).

Although in the United States, a defendant in a criminal trial is innocent until proved guilty, in France a defendant must be proved innocent. Therapists who view irrational thinking as the basis for pathological emotions and behavior take the French position. They place the burden of proof on the client whom they believe is thinking irrationally. If after your marriage breaks up, you say, "I will never find happiness with a lover," the therapist asks "Where is the proof that you will never find happiness with a lover?" You are required to prove your belief. The therapist, who obviously is implying the opposite, is not required to prove his or her belief. In fact, there are people who never found someone to love them and who were never in a happy long-term relationship. Had they made those statements, labeled irrational by Ellis, they would in fact have been correct.

Furthermore, though logicians define inductive arguments as those in which the premises provide some support, but not absolute support, for a conclusion, they do not define the word "some." Suppose you have been rejected by one lover, two, or perhaps three. How many must reject you to meet the criterion for "some support" for the inductive generalization? Conclusions are often judged to be irrational by cognitive therapists because the person has overgeneralized, but cognitive therapists, like logicians, do not propose how many occurrences permit generalization.

The fact that inductive reasoning may sometimes lead to false conclusions is no argument against it. The possibility of drawing false conclusions is inherent in the definition of inductive reasoning. But sometimes it is the only form of reasoning available to us.

DISCUSSION

Our aim here has been to show that economic models can be applied to suicidal behavior and, sometimes, lead to interesting conclusions about the nature of suicide. In particular, economic models have much to say about the rationality or irrationality of suicide, proposing a variety of criteria by which to make such judgments, criteria which supplement those proposed by psychologists.

REFERENCES

Becker, G. S. Irrational behavior and economic theory. *Journal of Political Economy*, 1962, 70, 1-13.

Becker, G. S., & Murphy, K. M. A theory of rational addiction. *Journal of Political Economy*, 1988, 96, 675-700.

Burns, D. *Feeling good*. New York: Morrow, 1980.

Dixit, A. K., & Pindyck, R. S. *Investment under uncertainty.* Princeton: Princeton University, 1994.

Ellis, A. *Humanistic psychotherapy.* New York: Julian, 1973.

Fehr, E., & Zych, P. K. The power of temptation. In G. Antonides & W. F. van Raaij (Eds.) *Proceedings of the IAREP/SABE Conference.* Rotterdam: Erasmus University, 1994, pp. 196-215.

Hamermesh, D. S., & Soss, N. An economic theory of suicide. *Journal of Political Economy,* 1974, 82, 83-98.

Lester, D., & Yang, B. Suicidal behavior and Becker's definition of irrationality. *Psychological Reports,* 1991, 68, 655-656.

Rosenthal, R. W. Suicide attempts and signaling games. *Mathematical Social Sciences,* 1993, 26, 25-33.

Wilber, C. G. Some thoughts on suicide: is it logical? *American Journal of Forensic Medicine & Pathology,* 1987, 8, 302-308.

Yeh, B. Y., & Lester, D. An economic model for suicide. In D. Lester, *Suicide as a learned behavior.* Springfield, IL: Charles Thomas, 1987, pp. 51-57.

PART 4:

EMPIRICAL STUDIES OF SUICIDE AND THE ECONOMY

CHAPTER 12

EMPLOYMENT, UNEMPLOYMENT AND SUICIDE

The relationship between working (or not working) and suicide has been of great interest to students of suicide. In particular, the association between unemployment and suicide has received more attention than that between suicide and other economic variables. In this chapter, we will examine the research that has been done on these topics and discuss some of the explanations which have been proposed.

TYPES OF RESEARCH DESIGN

Dooley and Catalano (1980) categorized research into the association between economic variables and behavior disorders as *individual* versus *aggregate* and as *cross-sectional* versus *time-series*.

Individual studies measure the variables in individuals. In individual cross-sectional research a sample of subjects is chosen, and the economic variable and the suicidal variable are measured in each person. In individual time-series studies of individuals, a group of subjects is followed up and changes in their economic status and their suicidal status noted.

Aggregate studies measure the economic and suicidal variables over regions. In aggregate cross-sectional studies, the economic status of a set of regions (nations, states or provinces, counties or city wards) is correlated with the suicide rate in those regions. In aggregate time-series studies, one region is chosen, typically a nation, and the variation of the economic variable and the suicide rate examined over time.

The relevant research into the association between unemployment and suicide has been conducted by psychologists, sociologists and economists, and their differing methodologies and perspectives has created a good deal of interdisciplinary criticism. The following review of the relationship between unemployment and suicide is based in large part on an extensive review of the literature prepared by Platt (1984), a medical sociologist.[20]

COMPLETED SUICIDE AND UNEMPLOYMENT

CROSS-SECTIONAL STUDIES: INDIVIDUALS

Platt (1984) located thirteen studies in which the extent of unemployment among samples of completed suicides was noted without, however, reporting unemployment among a suitable control group. The range of estimates was 3 percent to 69 percent, with a median of 23 percent.

Several studies have calculated the suicide rate among the unemployed. Sainsbury (1955) found a rate of 73 per 100,000 per year in London compared to a suicide rate in the general population of 14. Yap (1958) in Hong Kong and Kraft and Babigan (1976) in New York also have reported a higher suicide rate in the unemployed. However, in British Columbia, Cumming, et al. (1975) found the reverse for women aged 15-24 and for widowed women aged 45-64.

Platt located two case control studies of the association between unemployment and completed suicide (that is, where an appropriate comparison group was also studied). Robin, et al. (1968) found more unemployed males among suicides as compared to psychiatric control patients but the reverse for women. Roy (1982) found more unemployed males among suicides in Toronto (Canada) than among psychiatric controls, but this difference was not found for female suicides.

Platt noted that the various studies were difficult to compare because they may have used different definitions of unemployment. Although some

---

[20] It should be noted that close examination of the studies reviewed by Platt reveals that not all were on unemployment. Some were focussed on alternative economic indicators.

authors have noted the reasons for unemployment among their samples of suicides (for example, being fired/laid off, unable to find work, medical sickness, or psychiatric disorder), the better studies have not done so. Some authors have tried informally to assess whether unemployment played a role in the suicide, but such data are probably unreliable. Yap (1958) in Hong Kong judged that unemployment played a role in the suicide of 5 percent of the men, while Sainsbury (1955) in London judged that unemployment played a role in 73 percent of the suicides he studied.

Cause-and-effect conclusions cannot be drawn from these studies. It may be that unemployment increases the risk of suicide. Alternatively, it may be that individuals with a psychiatric illness are more vulnerable both to suicide and to unemployment (by being fired or by impulsively quitting).

TIME-SERIES STUDIES: INDIVIDUALS

Platt (1984) located eight studies of individuals studied over time. Three were retrospective, comparing the employment history of suicides and controls, and all found a stronger history of job loss and job instability in the suicides as compared to other groups.

Five of the studies were prospective. In this research design, employed and unemployed people are followed-up to see how many complete suicide. Four of the studies found a higher risk of suicide in those who are unemployed than in those who are employed, while one study found no significant differences. Two of these studies, however, were not focused solely on suicide and grouped suicidal deaths with accidents and homicides.

The most important feature of a well-designed follow-up study would be to focus on unemployed and employed individuals whose psychiatric health was known. This would enable the investigator to match subjects for psychiatric status and so eliminate this as a possible explanatory variable. Only two of the studies approached this design. Hagnell and Rorsman (1980) followed up psychiatric patients, but matched them only on demographic variables. They found more occupational problems in the suicides. Borg and Stahl (1982) also followed up psychiatric patients and matched them for diagnosis (though not for the severity of the disorder) and found no differences.

CROSS-SECTIONAL STUDIES: AGGREGATE

Platt (1984) identified nine studies in which suicide rates of regions had been correlated with the unemployment rates, covering seven tests of the association.

Five studies over regions of cities in the United Kingdom found no association while one found a positive association. These studies generally find that suicide rates are higher in areas of the city with overcrowding, people living alone, and high rates of social pathology. Unemployment is sometimes one of these associated variables. However, the impact of unemployment may not remain significant after a multiple regression analysis, and none of the studies reviewed by Platt used factor-analysis to explore the data set.

A study of 15 major labor market regions in Pennsylvania found a negative association between suicide rates and unemployment rates (Lester, 1970), but the impact of other social variables was not examined in this study.

A study of European nations found no association (Sainsbury, et al., 1980). However, unemployment rates did predict changes in the suicide rate in the following decade (higher unemployment rates predicted less of an increase), and changes in the unemployment rate after ten years were positively associated with changes in the suicide rate.

Rushing (1968) correlated the suicide and unemployment over sixty-four occupational groups in the United States and found a positive association only for the lower income groups.

More recently, Gove and Hughes (1980) found that the unemployment rate was positively associated with suicide rates in 389 American cities in 1970, South (1987) found a positive association over 292 Standard Metropolitan Statistical Areas, and Kowalski, et al. (1987) found a small positive association over American counties. Trovato (1986a) found a negative association over ethnic groups in Canada between the percentage of the group employed full-time and the suicide rate. (At the individual personal level, Bluestone, et al. [1981] reported that, when a plant closed in Detroit, eight of the two thousand workers laid off completed suicide soon thereafter).

On the other hand, Breault (1986) found that suicide rates and unemployment rates were not significantly associated over American states or counties. Charlton, et al. (1987) found no association between long-term unemployment rates and suicide rates in English regions, Renvoize and Clayden (1989) found no association over districts of Yorkshire in England, and Crombie (1989) found that changes in the unemployment rates in a small number of Scottish regions was not associated with changes in their suicide rates.

Data were available from a data set developed by the present authors to permit an examination of the relationship between unemployment and suicide rates in the forty-eight continental states of the United States in 1980. The Pearson correlation between suicide rates and unemployment rates are:

	suicide rates	
	male	female
unemployment rates		
male	-0.07	-0.10
female	-0.09	-0.12

and not significantly different from zero.

Data were also available from a data set developed by us for a study of suicide in 57 nations of the world with populations greater than one million in 1970. The suicide rate correlated significantly with the unemployment rate (Pearson $r = -0.37$, $p < 0.05$) but was much more strongly associated with the real gross domestic product per capita ($r = 0.62$). So, a partial correlation coefficient was calculated between the suicide rate and the unemployment rate controlling for the real gross domestic product per capita, and the suicide rate no longer correlated with the unemployment rate (partial $r = -0.10$).

Platt concluded that suicide and unemployment were probably unrelated in this type of study. He also noted that this research design does not permit cause-and-effect conclusions and typically fails to identify extraneous variables that might mediate any association that is uncovered between suicide and unemployment rates. Platt also noted that investigators often fell into the ecological fallacy in which an association at the aggregate level was thought to imply an association at the individual level (Robinson, 1950). The research here has also failed to take spatial autocorrelation into account (Odland, 1988) in which the geographic distribution of one or both of the correlational variables invalidates the use of regression techniques (which assume independent data points).

TIME-SERIES STUDIES: AGGREGATE

Platt (1984) identified over thirty studies of the temporal variation in suicide and unemployment rates or the economy. Seven of these studies did not report any statistical tests of the association, remaining content with simple visual charts. Thus, their results must be discarded.

Six studies have been conducted in Great Britain, but they have provided inconsistent results. Eleven studies have been conducted on the United States as a whole. Of these, six used years prior to 1933, a period when not all states reported mortality rates to the federal government. Thus, the region covered by mortality statistics from 1900 to 1933 changed periodically as more and more states cooperated with the federal government, and data from this period cannot be used. Five studies of the United States as a whole were methodologically sound, and all found a positive association between unemployment and suicide (Ahlburg and Schapiro, 1984; Brenner, 1977; Marshall, 1978; Marshall and Hodge, 1981; Stack, 1981).

Kreitman and Platt (1984) showed that the direction and size of the association in Great Britain were dependent upon the particular time period chosen and the method of suicide. In the United States, where the association between unemployment and suicide is generally found to be positive, Catalano, et al. (1982) found no association between monthly unemployment rates and suicide rates for both men and women in Monroe County, New York State.

In a study of eight nations from 1962 to 1976, Boor (1980) found a positive association for some age groups in four nations, nonsignificant associations in two nations and a negative association in one nation. Thus, the region chosen may also be important in determining the nature of the association.

Many studies on this issue have appeared since Platt's (1984) review of the research. A positive association between unemployment and suicide has been noted in Denmark (Iversen, et al., 1987), Norway (Stack, 1989), Sweden (Norstrom, 1988), the United States in a monthly analysis (Wasserman, 1984), Quebec (Cormier and Klerman, 1985), one county in Ohio (Filby and Eicher, 1983), the United States for 1948-1963 but not for 1964-1980 (Stack, 1987), and Scotland and Canada for men but not for women (Crombie, 1989; Trovato, 1986b). All of the above results were true for the simple correlations, but not all were confirmed when unemployment was thrown into a multiple regression analysis with other variables.

Thus, although the association may vary depending upon the nation used, in the United States from 1933 to the present time the association between unemployment rates and suicide rates does appear to be positive.

UNEMPLOYMENT AND ATTEMPTED SUICIDE

Platt (1984) also reviewed data on the association between unemployment and attempted suicide. It is noteworthy that there were far fewer studies on attempted suicides than on completed suicides. The one exception is that of individual cross-sectional studies. The majority of these report high levels of unemployment among parasuicides. For example, Kreitman (1973) calculated rates of attempted suicide among males in Edinburgh (Scotland) from 1968 to 1970 to be 92 per 100,000 per year for the employed and 2,444 for the unemployed.

However, unemployment is rarely given as a precipitating cause for attempts at suicide. For example, Morgan, et al. (1975) found that 51 percent of a sample of attempted suicides reported recent interpersonal conflict while only five percent reported concerns with work or unemployment.

Only two aggregate cross-sectional studies have been reported, both in British cites, and both reporting a positive association. Few individual or aggregate longitudinal studies have appeared, but Platt and Kreitman (1985) in an aggregate-longitudinal study in Edinburgh found a positive association between rates of attempted suicide and unemployment rates over time and, in addition, in a cross-sectional aggregate study, found a positive association over the wards of Edinburgh. Rates of attempted suicide were higher in unemployed men, especially if they had been unemployed for more than one year.

Thus, the evidence for attempted suicide is clearer. Although most of the studies have been conducted in Great Britain which limits their generality, there does appear to be a positive association between unemployment and attempted suicide.

EXPLANATIONS OF THE ASSOCIATION

Platt (1984) suggested two models for the relationship between suicide and unemployment.

(1) In a *causal* model, unemployment causes suicide.

(2) It has been clearly shown that the majority of suicides are psychiatrically disturbed (Lester, 1988a). In the *self-selection* model, those who are predisposed to suicide, typically by virtue of their psychiatric disturbance, are also more likely to become unemployed.

The results of a study by Hawton, et al. (1988) in England support this second possibility, though not unequivocally. They found that the rate of attempted suicide was higher in women if they had been unemployed, and especially high if they had been unemployed for a long time. A comparison of the unemployed attempters with the employed attempters revealed that the unemployed attempters had more often received psychiatric treatment in the past, were more likely to be alcoholics and had attempted suicide more in the past.

Similarly, Platt (1986; Platt and Duffy, 1986) found that attempted suicides who were unemployed were more likely to be drug abusers and to have a prior criminal record, though he found no differences between the unemployed and employed attempters in prior psychiatric treatment. Platt and Dyer (1987) found that unemployed attempters were more depressed and more hopeless than the employed attempters (though the two groups did not differ in suicidal intent or prior suicide attempts).

The process may be more complex. Unemployment may play a contributing role as a stressor in precipitating psychiatric illness or, directly, suicide. However, at the individual level, those who are unemployed may be more likely to develop a psychiatric illness. At the aggregate level, a society with poor opportunities for work may subject its citizens to higher levels of psychosocial stress, both for those who are employed (who may fear future unemployment) and for those already unemployed.

A more complicated model has been proposed by Dooley and Catalano (1980). Economic changes lead to social changes and to individually experienced life changes. Non-economic variables also lead to individually experienced life changes. In the next step, the social changes and the individually experienced life changes both lead either to individually experienced symptoms or to an asymptomatic adaptation.

The available evidence does not enable us to decide between these alternative models. We need individual longitudinal studies with the specific aim of testing these alternative hypotheses. A cohort of people must be psychiatrically evaluated, and then their work history and mortality documented over subsequent decades.

OCCUPATION AND SUICIDE

Suicide rates vary greatly with occupation. For example, Labovitz and Hagedorn (1971) found that self-employed managers and proprietors had the highest suicide rate in the United States in 1950, with policemen, detectives, sheriffs, bailiffs, marshals, and constables second. At the other end of the scale, clergymen had the lowest suicide rate. In California, Rose and Rosnow (1973) found a high suicide rate for physicians, chemists, dentists, pharmacists, musicians, and non-medical technicians and low rates for college teachers, clergymen, and social workers. Maris (1967) found higher suicide rates in service workers in Cook County, Illinois, (policemen, barbers, housekeepers, nurses, etc.) than in craftsmen (carpenters, tailors, etc.) or operatives (taxi drivers, assemblers, apprentices, etc.)

OCCUPATIONAL STATUS

In England, suicide has been reported to be more common in those of higher occupational status (Stengel, 1964), except for the elderly for whom the association is reversed. Suicide also appears to be more common in the higher social classes in New Zealand (Porterfield and Gibbs, 1960). In the United States, on the other hand, suicide has been reported to be more common in those of lower occupational status (Tuckman, et al., 1964; Maris, 1967).

OCCUPATIONAL PRESTIGE

Labovitz and Hagedorn (1971) found no association between the suicide rate of an occupational group and its prestige. Incidentally, Lester (1987, 1988b) found no association between the suicide rate of an occupational group in the United States and their median income or the number of people in that occupation.

Lampert, et al. (1984) found in Sacramento from 1925 to 1979 that suicide rates were higher in those occupations with less social status, such as farm laborers, general laborers, and service workers. Stack (1980) found a similar phenomenon in Detroit.

OTHER OCCUPATIONAL VARIABLES

Ahlburg and Schapiro (1984) examined the effects of the ratio of young/old labor force workers over time in the United States and found that the more younger people in the labor market, the higher the suicide rates of younger workers and older female workers and the lower the suicide rates of older male workers. In Canada over time, Labovitz and Brinkerhoff (1977) found that the percentage of white collar workers in the labor force was negatively associated with the suicide rate.

SUICIDE RATES IN PARTICULAR OCCUPATIONS

PSYCHOLOGISTS

Mausner and Steppacher (1973) found a lower suicide rate than expected for male psychologists but a higher rate than expected for female psychologists. The psychologists who committed suicide were less often married as compared to psychologists dying from other causes, and they used medications less than physicians who committed suicide.

POLICE

Several small studies have suggested that police officers have a high rate of suicide, and Lester (1978) reviewed available data to indicate that this does indeed seem to be a valid conclusion.

PHYSICIANS

Several investigators have reported higher suicide rates for physicians than for the adults in general. Rose and Rosnow (1973) found a high rate of suicide in California physicians. Steppacher and Mausner (1973) also found that male and female physicians had high suicide rates, with the female rate as high as the male rate. The females were younger and more often single. Pitts, et al. (1979) reported similar findings. Murray (1974) reported a high suicide rate for both male and female doctors in England, and for the wives of doctors too. Birmingham and Ward (1985) reported a high suicide rate in anesthesiologists. Bedeian (1982) reviewed the literature and found evidence for high suicide rates for physicians and pharmacists, but average rates for dentists and nurses. In Sweden, Arnetz, et al. (1987a, 1987b) found a high suicide rate in physicians but not in dentists and university faculty.

De Hart (1974) found a higher suicide rate for male physicians if they were aged thirty-five to sixty-five as compared to white males in general, but lower rates for physicians younger than thirty-four and older than seventy. Both Waltzer (1979) and Rich and Pitts (1979) found average rates for physicians.

The results seem to indicate a higher suicide rate for female physicians, but are less clear about a higher suicide rate in male physicians.

STUDENTS

Hawton, et al. (1978) found a higher suicide rate for students at Oxford University but a lower rate of attempted suicide. Although Iga (1971) claimed that students at Kyoto University had a high suicide rate, it appears comparable to that of the general population. Peck and Schrut (1971) found that students at elite universities in the United States had a high suicide rate while students in general had an average suicide rate. Leonard and Flinn (1972) found that music and psychology majors were more likely to report suicidal ideation than engineering and medical students.

CRISIS INTERVENTION WORKERS

Zung and Moore (1976) found that crisis intervention volunteers had a higher incidence of suicide attempts than hospital staff members, but not as high as psychiatric patients. Seiden and Borges (1974) found that suicide prevention volunteers were not as preoccupied with suicide and death as attempted suicides. When they did think of suicide, it was more often in response to physical problems rather than interpersonal problems.

OTHER OCCUPATIONS

High suicide rates have been reported in granite workers (Davis, et al., 1983), members of Equity (the actor's union) and the Screen Actors Guild (Depue, et al., 1985), veterinarians (Blair and Hayes, 1982), and workers in the tobacco industry (Blair, et al., 1983). Ragland and Berman (1987) reported a higher suicide rate in farmers and foresters than in truck drivers, and they noted that farmer suicide rates were especially high in years when the farm economy was in decline. Olsen and Lajer (1979) noted a higher proportion of deaths from suicide in Danish bricklayers than in carpenters, and they also noted that those committing suicide had more often experienced recent unemployment than those dying of natural deaths.

Mancuso and Locke (1972) found a high suicide rate for workers at a viscose rayon plant while deaths from other causes were as expected. They speculated that carbon disulfide may have played a role in precipitating suicidal behavior.

An average suicide rate has been reported for members of the boilermakers' union, except for shopfitters (Beaumont and Weiss, 1980).

DISCUSSION

One explanation of the suicide rates in different occupations focuses on the stress involved in some jobs. It has been argued, for example, that service occupations, such as counseling, make great psychological demands on the worker which may lead to a higher risk of suicide. It may be also that suicidal people are more attracted by some occupations than others (such as psychiatry and crisis intervention).

An alternative explanation focuses on the availability of lethal methods for self-destruction in some occupations (Clarke and Lester, 1989). Police officers own and carry guns. Physicians have easy access to lethal medications.

SUICIDE IN WORKING WOMEN

Men kill themselves at a higher rate than do women. Studies of suicide in the United States and around the world have indicated that the completed suicide rate is, in general, much higher than the suicide rate for women (Lester, 1984). However, in certain professions, women appear to have a higher suicide rate than their male counterparts.

Female chemists were found by Li (1969) to have a higher suicide rate than male chemists. Mausner and Steppacher (1973) reported a higher suicide rate than expected for female psychologists. Some recent studies (Craig and Pitts, 1968; Steppacher and Mausner, 1974; Pitts, et al., 1979) have uncovered what appears to be very high suicide rates for female physicians in the United States.

In a study that examined the factors behind the high rate of suicide of female physicians, Carlson and Miller (1981) noted that people who are at greatest risk for depressive disorder (and thereby at a higher risk of suicide) are in their 20s, 30s, and 40s. These are periods in the life of female physicians when the psychosocial stressors involved with medical training, career choice, and role conflicts are most salient. Those without a support system of colleagues and family are at even higher risk. The authors hypothesized that not only do female physicians have the intelligence and education to plan a suicide, but they also have the knowledge and means available to successfully kill themselves before the suicidal impulse subsides, leaving little margin for error or a change of mind. The same hypothesis may apply also to other female professionals, such as female psychologists and chemists.

WOMEN AND EMPLOYMENT

What is the impact for women of employment in general on their incidence of suicide? The question can be answered at two levels. One relates the employment of women to their mental health in general. The other examines the impact of work on their suicidal behavior.

Regarding the first issue, it has been found that work for women leads to reduced contact with their spouse and children (Staines and Pleck, 1983), reduced affection from and less harmony with their spouse (Geeken and Gove, 1983), and more guilt (Mortimer and London, 1984). Compared with other groups, married women with full-time jobs experience the highest tension; housewives show the least; married women working part-time are in-between (Michelson, 1985).

Baruch, et al. (1987), after reviewing the benefits and the costs of the employment of women, concluded that work is not always beneficial to women. The jobs most likely to involve stressors that impair health are those that demand a great deal but permit very little autonomy. Such jobs are typically low-level and low-paying ones.

However, some studies draw very different conclusions. A variety of well-controlled studies show significant mental and physical health differences that favor employed women over non-employed women (Merikangas, 1985; Verbrugge, 1982; Waldron and Herold, 1984).

Other research has investigated the incidence of suicide in employed and non-employed women. For example, Steffensmeier (1984) suggested that the increase in female suicide rates during the 1970s in the United States might have been related to changes over time in the degree of social integration and the role conflict of working women, responses to broad societal changes occurring during the 1960s and to the development of ideological support for an acceptance of role changes in the sexual, marital, and economic realms.

In a study of just four states in America, Alston (1986) found that the suicide rates of women were highest in moderately traditional occupations (where the percentage of women was 50 percent to 69 percent), lowest in the highly traditional occupations and in-between in the non-traditional occupations. In Georgia, Alston (1988) found that employed black women had a higher suicide rate than unemployed black women, while the reverse was true for white women. Alston also found ethnic differences in the suicide rate of women in different occupations in North Carolina.

In British Columbia (Canada), Cumming, et al. (1975) reported that married women who were employed had lower suicide rates than those not employed, and the same was true for women with other marital statuses.

FEMALES IN THE LABOR FORCE

It has been argued that the participation of females in the labor force is a source of conflict (Miley and Micklin, 1972; Newman, et al., 1973). Stack (1978) has suggested that this conflict may result in higher rates of suicide among married women due to the role conflict created between household and working responsibilities.

Theoretically, the participation of women in the labor force fits well with a theory of status integration and suicide proposed by Gibbs and Martin (1964). Gibbs and Martin felt that the degree to which the different statuses (or roles) held by people in a society were integrated (and free from conflict) would be related to the suicide rate. Stack (1978) used the participation of women in the labor force as an index of status integration.

Stack argued that, the more women participate in the labor force, the lower the status integration of the society and thus the higher the suicide rate.

Three studies on this topic focused on census tracts within major American cities. Newman, et al. (1973) found that census tracts with a higher participation rate of women in the labor force had higher overall suicide rates in both Atlanta and Chicago. However, Lester (1973; Diggory and Lester, 1976) failed to find any association in Buffalo, for the total suicide rate or for the male and female suicide rates. Breault (1986) found no association over the states of America and over counties, and Kowalski, et al. (1987) replicated the absence of an association over counties (but only for urban counties).

In a study of 45 nations, Stack (1978) found a positive association between the participation of women in the labor force and the overall suicide rate, even after controlling for the variables of industrialization and the rate of economic growth, and he has replicated this finding in other studies while Lester (1988c) has replicated it in a sample of only the industrialized nations. Vigderhous and Fishman (1977) found a negative association over nations between male-female occupational similarity and the female suicide rate, while the female professional labor force participation rate was not associated with female suicide rates.

Although Trovato (1987) found a positive association between female participation in the labor force and suicide over time in Canada, Labovitz and Brinkerhoff (1977) found no association. Davis (1981) reported a time-series analysis for the United States as a whole for 1950 to 1969 and found that female participation in the labor force, both overall and for married women, was positively associated with the female suicide rate but not with the male suicide rate, though Ahlburg (1985) reported a positive association only for those aged 15 to 24 years of age. Stack (1987) found a positive association between *mothers'* participation in the labor force and suicide over time in the United States, while Stack and Haas (1984) found no association.

Lester (1990) has questioned the social meaning of the variation in female participation in the labor force over regions. In the United States, female and male participation in the labor force are strongly associated with each other over the states, suggesting that female participation in the labor force is simply a reflection of other social factors such as the age structure of the population or the employment possibilities. Interestingly, over time in recent years, American male and female participation in the labor force have been negatively associated. Women have been working more often and men less often in successive years.

Yang and Lester (1988) reported a cross-sectional analysis over the states of America and found that the rate of married women working full-time or part-time did not have any association with the suicide rate of men or women. However, in a follow-up study (Yang and Lester, 1989) they found that the suicide rates of *married* men and *married* women were associated with the participation of married women in the labor force. The greater the proportion of married women working full-time and the smaller the proportion working part-time, the higher the suicide rate of married men and women. These associations were not found for the suicide rates of single, divorced, or widowed men and women.

Conclusions

The evidence in this chapter indicates the existence of an association between unemployment and suicidal behavior, but the factors affecting whether this association is found or not are not well understood. The evidence also indicates that the suicide rates of those in some occupations is higher than expected, but again there are several possible explanations for this, and research has not yet attempted to test them.

The evidence as to whether working is beneficial or detrimental for women is unclear. Aggregate studies have provided inconsistent results, while individual studies have so far indicated only that the topic is complex. While Cumming and her associates in Canada have found that working is associated with a reduced suicide rate in women, Alston in the United States has suggested that the association may depend upon the type of occupation.

REFERENCES

Ahlburg, D. A. The effects of strikes on suicide. *Sociological Focus*, 1985, 18, 29-36.

Ahlburg, D. A., & Schapiro, M. O. Socioeconomic ramifications of changing cohort size. *Demography*, 1984, 21, 97-108.

Alston, M. H. Occupation and suicide among women. *Issues in Mental Health Nursing*, 1986, 8, 109-119.

Alston, M. H. Occupational correlates of suicide in black and other nonwhite women. In D. Lester (Ed.) *Suicide '88*. Denver: American Association of Suicidology, 1988, 206.

Arnetz, B. B., Horte, L. G., Hedberg, A., & Malker, H. Suicide among Swedish dentists. *Scandinavian Journal of Social Medicine*, 1987a, 15, 243-246.

Arnetz, B. B., Horte, L. G., Hedberg, A., Theorell, T., Allander, E., & Malker, H. Suicide patterns among physicians related to other academics as well as to the general population. *Acta Psychiatrica Scandinavica*, 1987b, 75, 139-143.

Baruch, G. K., Biener, L., & Barnett, R. C. Women and gender in research on work and family stress. *American Psychologist*, 1987, 42, 130-136.

Beaumont, J. J., & Weiss, N. S. Mortality of welders, shopfitters and other metal trade workers in boilermakers local no 104, AFL-CIO. *American Journal of Epidemiology*, 1980, 112, 775-786.

Bedeian, A. Suicide and occupation. *Journal of Vocational Behavior*, 1982, 21, 206-223.

Birmingham, P., & Ward, R. A high risk suicide group. *American Journal of Psychiatry*, 1985, 142, 1225-1226.

Blair, A. Berney, B. W., Heid, M. F., & White, D. W. Causes of death among workers in the tobacco industry. *Archives of Environmental Health*, 1983, 38, 223-228.

Blair, A., & Hayes, H. Mortality patterns among US veterinarians. *International Journal of Epidemiology*, 1982, 11, 391-397.

Bluestone, B., Harrison, B., & Baker, L. *Corporate flight.* Washington, DC: Progressive Alliance, 1981.

Borg, S. E., & Stahl, M. Prediction of suicide. *Acta Psychiatrica Scandinavica,* 1982, 65, 221-232.

Boor, M. Relationships between unemployment rates and suicide rates in eight countries, 1962-1976. *Psychological Reports,* 1980, 47, 1095-1101.

Breault, K. D. Suicide in America. *American Journal of Sociology,* 1986, 92, 628-656.

Brenner, M. H. Health costs and benefits of economic policy. *International Journal of Health Services,* 1977, 7, 581-623.

Carlson, G. A., & Miller, D. C. Suicide, affective disorder, and women physicians. *American Journal of Psychiatry,* 1981, 138, 1330-1335.

Catalano, R. A., Dooley, D., & Jackson, R. Selecting a time-series strategy. Unpublished, 1982.

Charlton, J. R., Bauer, R., Thalchore, A., Silver, R., & Aristidou, M. Unemployment and mortality. *Journal of Epidemiology & Community Health,* 1987, 41, 107-113.

Clarke, R. V., & Lester, D. *Suicide: closing the exits.* New York: Springer-Verlag, 1989.

Cormier, H. J., & Klerman, G. L. Unemployment and male-female labor force participation as determinants of changing suicide rates of males and females in Quebec. *Social Psychiatry,* 1985, 20, 109-114.

Craig, A. G., & Pitts, F. N. Suicide by physicians. *Diseases of the Nervous System,* 1968, 29, 763-772.

Crombie, I. K. Trends in suicide and unemployment in Scotland, 1976-1986. *British Medical Journal,* 1989, 298, 782-784.

Cumming, E., Lazar, C., & Chisholm, L. Suicide as an index of role strain among employed and not employed married women in British Columbia. *Canadian Review of Sociology & Anthropology,* 1975, 12, 463-469.

Davis, L. K., Wegman, D. H., Monson, R. R., & Froines, J. Mortality experience of Vermont granite workers. *American Journal of Industrial Medicine,* 1983, 4, 705-724.

Davis, R. Female labor force participation, status integration and suicide, 1950-1969. *Suicide & Life-Threatening Behavior*, 1981, 11, 111-123.

De Hart, C. Suicide by physicians. *Journal of the Maine Medical Association*, 1974, 65(2), 32-33.

Depue, R. H., Kagey, B. T., & Heid, M. F. A proportional mortality study of the acting profession. *American Journal of Industrial Medicine*, 1985, 8, 57-66.

Diggory, J. D., & Lester, D. Suicide rates of men and women. *Omega*, 1976, 7, 95-101.

Dooley, D., & Catalano, R. Economic change as a cause of behavioral disorder. *Psychological Bulletin*, 1980, 87, 450-468.

Filby, R. G., & Eicher, G. M. Unemployment and the suicide rate. *Ohio State Medical Journal*, 1983, 79, 837-848.

Geeken, M., & Gove, W. R. *At home and at work.* Beverly Hills: Sage, 1983.

Gibbs, J. P., & Martin, W. T. *Status integration and suicide.* Eugene, OR: University of Oregon Press, 1964.

Gove, W. R., & Hughes, M. Re-examining the ecological fallacy. *Social Forces*, 1980, 58, 1157-1177.

Hagnell, O., & Rorsman, B. Suicide in the Lundby study. *Neuropsychobiology*, 1980, 6, 319-332.

Hawton, K., Crowle, J., Simkin, S., & Bancroft, J. Attempted suicide and suicide among Oxford University students. *British Journal of Psychiatry*, 1978, 132, 506-509.

Hawton, K., Fagg, J., & Simkin, S. Female unemployment and attempted suicide. *British Journal of Psychiatry*, 1988, 152, 632-637.

Iga, M. College students' suicide and value orientations in Japan. American Association of Suicidology, Washington, DC, 1971.

Iversen, L., Andersen, O., Andersen, P. K., Christoffersen, K., & Keiding, N. Unemployment and mortality in Denmark, 1970-1980. *British Medical Journal*, 1987, 295, 879-884.

Kowalski, G. S. Faupel, C. E., & Starr, P. D. Urbanism and suicide. *Social Forces*, 1987, 66, 85-101.

Kraft, D. P., & Babigan, H. M. Suicide by persons with and without psychiatric contacts. *Archives of General Psychiatry*, 1976, 33, 209-215.

Kreitman, N. Social and clinical aspects of suicide and attempted suicide. In A. Forrest (Ed.) *A companion to psychiatric studies.* Edinburgh: Churchill Livingston, 1973, volume 1, 38-63.

Kreitman, N., & Platt, S. Suicide, unemployment and domestic gas detoxification in Great Britain. *Journal of Epidemiology & Community Health*, 1984, 38, 1-6.

Labovitz, S., & Brinkerhoff, M. Structural changes and suicide in Canada. *International Journal of Comparative Sociology*, 1977, 18, 254-267.

Labovitz, S., & Hagedorn, R. An analysis of suicide rates among occupational categories. *Sociological Inquiry*, 1971, 41, 67-72.

Lampert, D., Bourque, L., & Kraus, J. Occupational status and suicide. *Suicide & Life-Threatening Behavior*, 1984, 14, 254-269.

Leonard, C. V., & Flinn, D. Suicidal ideation and behavior in youthful nonpsychiatric populations. *Journal of Consulting & Clinical Psychology*, 1972, 38, 366-371.

Lester, D. Suicide and unemployment. *Archives of Environmental Health*, 1970, 20, 277-278.

Lester, D. Completed suicide and females in the labor force. *Psychological Reports*, 1973, 32, 730.

Lester, D. Suicide in police officers. *Police Chief*, 1978, 45(4), 17.

Lester, D. Occupational prestige and rates of suicide and homicide. *Perceptual & Motor Skills*, 1987, 64, 398.

Lester, D. *The biochemical basis of suicide.* Springfield: Thomas, 1988a.

Lester, D. Social deviancy and suicide. *Psychological Reports*, 1988b, 63, 968.

Lester, D. Economic factors and suicide. *Journal of Social Psychology*, 1988c, 128, 245-248.

Lester, D. Women in the labor force and suicide. *Psychological Reports*, 1990, 66, 194.

Li, F. B. Suicide among chemists. *Archives of Environmental Health*, 1969, 19, 518-520.

Mancuso, T., & Locke, B. Carbon disulphide as a cause of suicide. *Journal of Occupational Medicine*, 1972, 14, 595-606.

Maris, R. Suicide, status and mobility in Chicago. *Social Forces*, 1967, 46, 246-256.

Marshall, J. R. Changes in aged white male suicide. *Journal of Gerontology*, 1978, 33, 763-768.

Marshall, J. R., & Hodge, R. W. Durkheim and Pierce on suicide and economic change. *Social Science Research*, 1981, 10, 101-114.

Mausner, J., & Steppacher, R. Suicide in professionals. *American Journal of Epidemiology*, 1973, 98, 436-445.

Merikangas, K. Sex differences in depression. Conference on Mental Health in Social Context, Cambridge, MA, 1985.

Michelson, W. *From sun to sun.* Totowa, NJ: Rowman & Allanheld, 1985.

Miley, J., & Micklin, M. Structural change and the Durkheimian legacy. *American Journal of Sociology*, 1972, 78, 657-673.

Morgan, H. G., Burns-Cox, C. J., Pocock, H., & Pottle, S. Deliberate self-harm. *British Journal of Psychiatry*, 1975, 127, 564-574.

Mortimer, J. T., & London, J. The varying linkages of work and family. In P. Voydanoff (Ed.) *Work and family.* Palo Alto, CA: Mayfield, 1984, 20-35.

Murray, R. Psychiatric illness in doctors. *Lancet*, 1974, 1, 1211-1213.

Newman, J., Whittemore, K., & Newman, H. Women in the labor force and suicide. *Social Problems*, 1973, 21, 220-230.

Norstrom, T. Deriving relative risks from aggregate data. *Journal of Epidemiology & Community Health*, 1988, 42, 336-340.

Odland, J. *Spatial autocorrelation.* Beverly Hills: Sage, 1988.

Olsen, J., & Lajer, M. Violent death and unemployment in two trade unions in Denmark. *Social Psychiatry*, 1979, 14, 139-145.

Peck, M., & Schrut, A. Suicidal behavior among college students. *HSMHA Health Reports*, 1971, 86, 149-156.

Pitts, F., Scholler, A., Rich, C., & Pitts, A. Suicide among US women physicians, 1967-1972. *American Journal of Psychiatry*, 1979, 136, 694-696.

Platt, S. D. Unemployment and suicidal behavior. *Social Science & Medicine*, 1984, 19, 93-115.

Platt, S. D. Clinical and social characteristics of male parasuicides. *Acta Psychiatrica Scandinavica*, 1986, 74, 24-31.

Platt, S. D., & Duffy, J. C. Social and clinical correlates of unemployment in two cohorts of male parasuicides. *Social Psychiatry*, 1986, 21, 17-24.

Platt, S. D., & Dyer, J. A. Psychological correlates of unemployment among male parasuicides in Edinburgh. *British Journal of Psychiatry*, 1987, 151, 27-32.

Platt, S. D., & Kreitman, N. Parasuicide and unemployment among men in Edinburgh, 1968-1982. *Psychological Medicine*, 1985, 15, 113-123.

Porterfield, A. L., & Gibbs, J. P. Occupational prestige and social mobility of suicides in New Zealand. *American Journal of Sociology*, 1960, 66, 147-152.

Ragland, J. D., & Berman, A. L. Farm crisis and suicide. In R. Yufit (Ed.) *Proceedings of the 20th Annual Meeting of the American Association of Suicidology*. Denver: American Association of Suicidology, 1987, 102-103.

Renvoize, E., & Clayden, D. Suicide and unemployment. *British Medical Journal*, 1989, 298, 1180.

Rich, C., & Pitts, F. Suicide by male physicians during a five year period. *American Journal of Psychiatry*, 1979, 136, 1089-1090.

Robin, A. A., Brooke, E. M., & Freeman-Browne, D. L. Some aspects of suicide in psychiatric patients in Southend. *British Journal of Psychiatry*, 1968, 114, 739-747.

Robinson, W. S. Ecological correlations and the behavior of individuals. *American Sociological Review*, 1950, 15, 351-357.

Rose, K., & Rosnow, I. Physicians who kill themselves. *Archives of General Psychiatry*, 1973, 29, 800-805.

Roy, A. Risk factors for suicide in psychiatric patients. *Archives of General Psychiatry*, 1982, 39, 1089-1095.

Rushing, W. A. Income, unemployment and suicide. *Sociological Quarterly*, 1968, 9, 493-503.

Sainsbury, P. *Suicide in London*. London: Chapman & Hall, 1955.

Sainsbury, P., Jenkins, J., & Levey, A. The social correlates of suicide in Europe. In R. Farmer & S. Hirsch (Eds.) *The suicide syndrome.* London: Croom Helm, 1980, 38-53.

Seiden, R. H., & Borges, S. Rescuers and the rescued. *Proceedings of the 7th International Congress for Suicide Prevention.* Amsterdam: Swets & Zeitlinger, 1974, 526-535.

South, S. J. Metropolitan migration and social problems. *Social Science Quarterly,* 1987, 68, 3-18.

Stack, S. Suicide. *Social Forces,* 1978, 57, 644-653.

Stack, S. Occupational status and suicide. *Aggressive Behavior,* 1980, 6, 233-234.

Stack, S. Divorce and suicide. *Journal of Family Issues,* 1981, 2, 77-90.

Stack, S. The effects of female participation in the labor force on suicide. *Sociological Forum,* 1987, 2, 257-277.

Stack, S. The impact of divorce on suicide in Norway, 1951-1980. *Journal of Marriage & the Family,* 1989, 51, 229-238.

Stack, S., & Haas, A. The effect of unemployment duration on national suicide rates, 1948-1982. *Sociological Focus,* 1984, 17, 17-29.

Staines, G. L., & Pleck, J. H. *The impact of work schedules on the family.* Ann Arbor: Institute for Social Research, 1983.

Steffensmeier, R. H. Suicide and the contemporary woman. *Sex Roles,* 1984, 10, 613-631.

Stengel, E. *Suicide and attempted suicide.* Baltimore: Penguin, 1964.

Steppacher, R., & Mausner, J. Suicide in male and female physicians. *Journal of the American Medical Association,* 1974, 228, 323-328.

Trovato, F. Suicide and ethnic factors in Canada. *International Journal of Social Psychiatry,* 1986a, 32(3), 55-64.

Trovato, F. A time-series analysis of international migration and suicide mortality in Canada. *International Journal of Social Psychiatry,* 1986b, 32(2), 38-40.

Trovato, F. A longitudinal analysis of divorce and suicide in Canada. *Journal of Marriage & the Family,* 1987, 49, 193-203.

Tuckman, J., Youngman, W. F., & Kreizman, G. Occupation and suicide. *Industrial Medicine & Surgery,* 1964, 33, 818-820.

Verbrugge, L. M. Women: social roles and health. In P. Berman and E. Ramey (Eds.) *Women: a developmental perspective.* Bethesda, MD: NIH, 1982, 49-78.

Vigderhous, G., & Fishman, G. Sociometric determinants of female suicide rates. *International Review of Modern Sociology,* 1977, 7, 199-211.

Waldron, I., & Herold, J. Employment, attitudes toward employment and women's health. Society of Behavioral Medicine, Philadelphia, 1984.

Waltzer, H. Physicians. In L. Hankoff and B. Einsidler (Eds.) *Suicide.* Littleton, MA: PSG, 1979, 323-333.

Wasserman, I. M. A longitudinal analysis of the linkage between suicide, unemployment and marital dissolution. *Journal of Marriage & the Family,* 1984, 46, 853-859.

Yang, B., & Lester, D. The participation of females in the labor force and rates of personal violence (suicide and homicide). *Suicide & Life-Threatening Behavior,* 1988, 18, 270-278.

Yang, B., & Lester, D. The association between working and personal violence (suicide and homicide) in married men and women. *Proceedings of the Annual Meeting of the Pennsylvania Economic Association.* University Park: Pennsylvania State University, 1989, 343-50.

Yap, P. M. Suicide in Hong Kong. *Journal of Mental Science,* 1958, 104, 266-301.

Zung, W., & Moore, J. Suicide potential in a normal adult population. *Psychosomatics,* 1976, 17, 37-41.

CHAPTER 13

RESEARCH ON OTHER ECONOMIC VARIABLES

There have been several studies on other economic variables (besides those on unemployment and female participation in the labor force reviewed in the previous chapter), and this research will be reviewed here.

GROSS NATIONAL PRODUCT PER CAPITA

Stack (1983) found that the gross national product per capita was positively associated with the suicide rate in nations of the world, while Lester (1987b) found that the association failed to reach statistical significance for eighteen industrialized nations (though it remained positive).

Stack (1982) found that the increase in the gross national product per capita was also positively associated with the suicide rates of nations. Abe, et al. (1986) found that the annual growth in the gross national product per capita of nations over a ten-year period was associated with a decrease in the seasonal variation in suicide rates over that same period in a sample of nations. In Japan, the gross national product per capita itself was associated over time with a decrease in the seasonality of suicide (Abe, 1987), but Lester (1993a) failed to find the same phenomenon in the United States.

INDUSTRIALIZATION

Stack (1985) examined the association over time between industrialization and suicide rates in eighteen nations. The association was positive in seven, negative in four and not significant in seven, showing that generalizations cannot be drawn about the association. On the other hand, Stack and Danigelis (1985) found that the time series association between the male/female suicide rate ratio and modernization (an index of urbanization, industrialization and education) was negative in sixteen of the seventeen nations studied (and statistically significant in fourteen of these nations).

INCOME

Stack (1980) found that median family income was not associated with suicide rates of the states of America (although Zimmerman [1987] reported a positive association). Breault (1986) found no association over counties (although Kowalski, et al. [1987] found that effect was negative for urban counties if a suitable set of social variables was placed into a multiple regression). South (1987) found no association over standard metropolitan statistical areas, and Gove and Hughes (1980) found no association over cities. Araki and Murata (1986) found that low income was associated over Japanese prefectures with higher suicide rates but only for middle-aged men.

Ahlburg (1985) found that real annual income in the United States was associated over time negatively for older men (aged 45 to 64), but positively for elderly women; however, another study (Ahlburg and Schapiro, 1984) found no association for overall suicide rates.

In a study of nations, Ellner (1977) applied a factor analysis to a large set of social indicators and found that one of the five factors had suicide rates loaded on it highly. This factor also had a high loading for the income level of the nations. However, it is impossible to be sure in this type of statistical analysis whether income level is the important variable since nine others variables were also loaded on the same factor.

In time series studies, Brenner (1977, 1983) found that the suicide rate was negatively association with per capita income in England and Wales and in Scotland, while the association was not significantly different from zero in the United States. In a time series study in Taiwan, Li (1971) found that per capita income was negatively related to suicide rates.

INCOME INEQUALITY

Lester (1987a) found no association across nations of the world between the Gini index of income inequality and suicide rates. Kowalski, et al. (1987) found a significant positive effect of income inequality on the suicide rates of urban American counties (but not for rural counties) if they placed income inequality and a suitable set of social indicators into a multiple regression analysis.

ECONOMIC SEX EQUALITY

Stack (1983) found that economic sex equality was positive associated with the overall suicide rate in the nations of the world, while Lester (1987b) found that the association did not reach statistical significance in a sample of industrialized nations.

TECHNOLOGICAL DEVELOPMENT

Lester (1989) found that technological growth (as measured by energy consumption) was not related to the suicide rates of nations of the world, but changes in the division of labor (that is, in the distribution of occupations in the country) were positively associated with suicide rates.

Labovitz and Brinkerhoff (1977) found that the relative percentage of secondary (versus primary) industries in Canada was positively associated with suicide rates over time.

URBANIZATION

Stack (1982a) found that the degree of urbanization in nations of the world was not associated with their suicide rate. Breault (1986) and Zimmerman (1987) found no association over the states or counties of America, although Kowalski, et al. (1987) reported a significant negative correlation over counties. In Canada, however, urbanization was positively associated with suicides rates over time (Labovitz and Brinkerhoff, 1977).

PUBLIC WELFARE EXPENDITURES

Zimmerman (1987) found that the per capita expenditure on public welfare (as well as mental health and overall per capita taxes) was negatively associated with the states' suicide rates (although the association was no longer significant when expenditures were put into a multiple regression with other social indicators).

BUSINESS ACTIVITY

Wasserman (1984) examined the association between monthly measures of the United States suicide rate and the Ayres business index. From 1910 to 1920 there was no association, but from 1924 to 1939 the association was negative.

Brenner (1977) found that inflation was positively related to the suicide rate in the United States over time. In England and Wales and in Scotland, the suicide rate was associated with bankruptcies (Brenner, 1983).

Munson (1968) correlated a variety of measures of business activity (such as the per capita value added by manufacturing and the per capita retail sales) with suicide rates over the counties in Ohio and in general found a negative association.

STRIKES

Stack (1982b) found that the suicide rate of nations of the world was negatively associated with strike volume and size, but not strike duration. (The associations were stronger for female suicide rates than for male suicide rates.) Lester (1988) reported this negative association on a reduced sample of eighteen industrialized nations for strike volume and duration, but not for size. Ahlburg (1985) found no association between strike activity and suicide rates *over time* in the United States.

THE MISERY INDEX

Economists have used the term "misery index" to describe the sum of the inflation and unemployment rates. Yang and Lester (1992) found that the misery index was strongly associated with the suicide in the United States from 1939 to 1986; however, the more important component of the index for predicting suicide rates was the unemployment rate rather than the inflation rate.

Lester (1993b) examined a misery index based on changes in inflation, unemployment, interest rates and shortfall in gross national product growth, an index which was calculated for each Presidential term from Truman (1949-1952) to Reagan (1985-1989). The average suicide rate during this series of Presidential terms was not associated with the misery index for the terms.

DISCUSSION

The research reviewed in this chapter has covered a wide variety of economic variables, but so far, few studies have been subjected to replication. Thus, it is difficult to judge the reliability of the findings. However, the results do suggest interesting areas for subsequent research, and it is to be hoped that future research will identify the reliable findings and test alternative explanations for them.

REFERENCES

Abe, K. Secular trends of suicide seasonality. *Progress in Biometeorology*, 1987, 5, 205-212.

Abe, K., Egashira, K., & Suzuki, T. Suicide seasonality and economic growth. *Stress Medicine*, 1986, 2, 79-81.

Ahlburg, D. A. The effects of strikes on suicide. *Sociological Focus*, 1985, 18, 29-36.

Ahlburg, D. A., & Schapiro, M. Socioeconomic ramifications of changing cohort size. *Demography*, 1984, 21, 97-108.

Araki, S., & Murata, K. Factors affecting suicide in young, middle-aged and elderly men. *Journal of Biosocial Science*, 1986, 18, 103-108.

Breault, K. D. Suicide in America. *American Journal of Sociology*, 1986, 92, 628-656.

Brenner, M. H. Health costs and benefits of economic policy. *International Journal of Health Sciences*, 1977, 7, 581-623.

Brenner, M. H. Mortality and economic instability. *International Journal of Health Services*, 1983, 13, 563-620.

Ellner, M. Research on international suicide. *International Journal of Social Psychiatry*, 1977, 23, 187-194.

Gove, W. R., & Hughes, M. Re-examining the ecological fallacy. *Social Forces*, 1980, 58, 1157-1177.

Kowalski, G. S., Faupel, C. E., & Starr, P. D. Urbanism and suicide. *Social Forces*, 1987, 66, 85-101.

Labovitz, S., & Brinkerhoff, M. Structural changes and suicide in Canada. *International Journal of Comparative Sociology*, 1977, 18, 254-267.

Lester, D. Relation of income inequality to suicide and homicide rates. *Journal of Social Psychology*, 1987a, 127, 101-102.

Lester, D. Cross-national correlations among religion, suicide and homicide. *Sociology & Social Research*, 1987b, 71, 103-104.

Lester, D. Strikes, suicide and homicide. *International Journal of Contemporary Sociology*, 1988, 25, 9-14.

Lester, D. Association of population growth, technological development and social integration on rates of personal violence (suicide and homicide). *Psychological Reports*, 1989, 64, 462.

Lester, D. Seasonality in suicide and economic growth. *Perceptual & Motor Skills*, 1993a, 77, 10.

Lester, D. Suicide and homicide rates during Presidential terms as a function of economic conditions. *Psychological Reports*, 1993b, 73, 50.

Li, W. L. A comparative study of suicide. *International Journal of Comparative Sociology*, 1971, 12, 281-286.

Munson, B. E. Relationship between economic activity and critical community dimensions. *American Journal of Economics & Sociology*, 1968, 27, 225-237.

South, S. J. Metropolitan migration and social problems. *Social Science Quarterly*, 1987, 68, 3-18.

Stack, S. The effects of interstate migration on suicide. *International Journal of Social Psychiatry*, 1980, 26(1), 17-25.

Stack, S. Aging and suicide. *International Journal of Contemporary Sociology*, 1982a, 19(3/4) 125-138.

Stack, S. The effect of strikes on suicide. *Sociological Focus*, 1982, 15, 135-146.

Stack, S. The effect of religious commitment on suicide. *Journal of Health & Social Behavior*, 1983, 24, 362-374.

Stack, S. Economic development, religion and lethal aggression. *Deviant Behavior*, 1985, 6, 233-236.

Stack, S., & Danigelis, N. Modernization and the sex differential in suicide, 1919-1972. *Comparative Sociological Research*, 1985, 8, 203-216.

Wasserman, I. The influence of economic business cycles on US suicide rates. *Suicide & Life-Threatening Behavior*, 1984, 14, 143-156.

Yang, B., & Lester, D. The misery index and an index of misery. *Atlantic Economic Journal*, 1992, 20(3), 98.

Zimmerman, S. L. State-level public policy as a predictor of individual and family well-being. *Women & Health*, 1987, 12(3/4), 161-188.

CHAPTER 14

THE QUALITY OF LIFE AND PERSONAL VIOLENCE

C ommon sense suggests that, as we improve conditions in the world, people should be much happier. If we can eliminate poverty and oppression such as sexism and racism, if we clean up the environment, if we improve the educational and cultural offerings for our citizens, if we do all this, then we should be much happier. Then, as the quality of life declines, life should be less worth living.

In contrast, Henry and Short (1954) have argued that when external conditions are bad, we have a clear source to blame for our own misery, and this makes us outwardly angry rather than inwardly angry or depressed. When times are good, there is no clear external source of blame for our misery, and so we are more likely to become inwardly angry or depressed and less likely to be outwardly angry. Henry and Short would argue that a higher quality of life would lead to higher rates of suicide and lower rates of homicide, whereas a lower quality of life would lead to lower rates of suicide and higher rates of homicide.

These contrasting ideas lead to opposite predictions, and several sets of data exist to test the predictions.

STATES OF AMERICA

Angoff and Mencken (1931) rated the states of America for the quality of life using one hundred objective measures of wealth, education, health, public order, and the overall quality of life. The correlations between the rates of personal violence in the states and these indices were as follows (Lester, 1985a):

	suicide rate	homicide rate
wealth	0.65*	-0.57*
education	0.62*	-0.62*
health	0.47*	-0.74*
public order	0.17	-0.87*
overall quality of life	0.51*	-0.74*

Thus it can be seen clearly that suicide rates were higher in the states with a higher quality of life while homicide rates were lower in those states. Furthermore, these associations were found for the particular sub-index of wealth.

Additional data can be found in Porterfield and Talbert (1948). These authors constructed an index of social well-being from indices of economic welfare, education and culture, living conditions (housing), medical facilities, voting, and general health for the states in 1940. Lester (1986) correlated these indices with rates of personal violence and the results were as follows:

	suicide rate	homicide rate
overall quality of life	0.49*	-0.72*
economic index	0.62*	-0.61*
housing index	0.23	-0.57*
suffrage index	0.60*	-0.56*
education index	0.59*	-0.74*
medical facilities index	0.39*	-0.62*
health index	0.30*	-0.78*

* statistically significant

It can be seen that these data are consistent with those from 1931, and the economic index correlates positively with suicide rates and negatively with homicide rates as before.

Incidentally, surveys were taken of residents in the nine major regions of the United States in 1980 asking them how satisfied they were with life, but these ratings were not associated with the suicide rates of the regions (Lester, 1987).

STANDARD METROPOLITAN STATISTICAL AREAS

Boyer and Savageau (1981) rated the major metropolitan areas of the United States for various aspects of the quality of life. Lester (1985b) correlated these scores with rates of personal violence in the fifty largest metropolitan areas. The results were as follows:

	suicide rate	homicide rate
overall quality of life	-0.05	0.03
economic conditions	0.62*	0.16
crime	-0.43*	-0.58*
education	-0.31*	-0.28*
climate and terrain	0.04	-0.08
housing	-0.03	0.24*
health care and environment	-0.17	0.21
transportation	-0.06	0.26*
recreation	0.22	-0.05
arts	-0.12	0.13

Overall, these data are not supportive of either hypothesis. The quality of life was not related to rates of personal violence. However, suicide rates

---

* statistically significant

were higher in those metropolitan areas where the economic index was higher, in line with Henry and Short's theory.

Lester (1989) correlated ratings of the overall quality of life in American cities in 1930 with their suicides rates and found a positive association. Thus, either the composition of the quality of life index is critical in determining the result of the study or the association is not found consistently in every era (or both).

NATIONS OF THE WORLD

Estes (1984) has developed an index of social progress (or the quality of life) based upon a variety of social and political factors in the nations of the world in 1969: education, health status, women's status, defense effort, economy, demographics (birth rate), geography (land use and natural disasters), political stability, political participation, cultural diversity, and welfare effort.

Table 14.1 The Association between the Quality of Life and Rates of Personal Violence

	18 nations		43 nations	
	suicide rate	*homicide rate*	*suicide rate*	*homicide rate*
quality of life	0.30	-0.68***	0.57***	-0.50***
education	-0.16	0.12	0.38**	-0.58***
health	0.25	-0.28	0.46***	-0.63***
women's status	-0.23	0.11	0.34*	-0.31*
defense effort	0.24	-0.41*	0.16	0.17
economy	0.34	0.36	0.22	-0.07
demography	0.57**	-0.68***	0.61***	-0.56***
geography	0.06	-0.87***	0.21	-0.46***
political stability	0.43*	-0.15	0.16	0.11
political participation	-0.29	0.14	0.18	-0.17
cultural diversity	0.07	-0.22	-0.04	-0.21
welfare effort	0.08	-0.54*	0.49***	-0.48***

* one-tailed $p < 0.05$ ** one-tailed $p < 0.01$ *** one-tailed $p < 0.001$

Lester (1984) found that suicide rates correlated positively with the overall quality of life in 43 nations with available data, while homicide rates correlated negatively with the quality of life (see Table 14.1). These results stood up when the gross natural product per capita of the nations was controlled for by use of partial correlation coefficients. Thus, this initial analysis of Estes's data confirmed the prediction from Henry and Short rather than the prediction from common sense.

Estes, however, used several components for his overall rating of the quality of life, including education, health status and women's status. (A complete list of the components is presented in Appendix A.) Lester (1990) examined the relationship between these components and rates of personal violence in detail.

The data were first analyzed for a sample of 43 nations whose populations in 1980 were greater than one million and for which data were available. The Pearson correlations between the components of the quality of life and rates of personal violence for 1980 are shown in Table 14.1.

For the complete sample of 43 nations, only five of the eleven components of the quality of life index correlated with suicide rates, and only six of the components correlated with homicide rates. Interestingly, defense efforts, the economy, political stability, political participation and cultural diversity were not correlated with rates of personal violence. The strongest correlates were the education, health, and demographic components.

For the reduced sample of industrialized nations, even fewer components correlated with the rates of personal violence, though the associations were more consistent for homicide rates than for suicide rates.

For the total sample of 43 nations, a factor analysis of the components of the quality of life (using SPSSX with a PC extraction and a varimax rotation) identified four factors, only one of which correlated with rates of personal violence (see Table 14.2). This factor (Factor I) had the strongest loadings from health, demography, welfare, and education. A similar factor analysis for the 18 industrialized nations identified five factors, only one of which correlated with homicide rates (see Table 14.3). This factor had high loadings from geography, welfare effort, and demography.

Table 14.2 The Association between Components of the Quality of Life
and Rates of Personal Violence for 43 Nations in 1980

	Factor			
	I	*II*	*III*	*III*
education	0.80*	-0.10	0.02	-0.07
health	0.91*	-0.11	0.01	-0.09
women's status	0.68*	-0.23	0.20	0.34
defense effort	-0.04	0.06	0.80*	0.26
economy	0.27	0.07	0.61*	-0.50*
demography	0.90*	0.06	0.01	-0.04
geography	0.46*	0.43*	0.33	0.12
political stability	-0.10	0.79*	0.24	-0.06
political participation	0.50*	-0.65*	0.21	-0.25
cultural diversity	0.12	0.09	0.12	0.80*
welfare effort	0.86*	-0.11	0.01	0.25
percent of variance	38%	13%	11%	10%
correlation with				
suicide rate	0.55#	0.20	0.17	-0.07
homicide rate	-0.65#	-0.11	0.22	-0.07

* a high loading on the factor (greater than 0.40)
# one-tailed significance less than 0.001

Examination of changes in these variables revealed that changes in the quality of life from 1969 to 1979 were not associated with suicide rates in 1980 or changes in suicide rates during the 1970s (see Table 14.4). However, for the industrialized nations, increases in the quality of life were associated with greater increases in the homicide rates during the 1970s and higher homicide rates in 1980.

These results indicated that the general associations identified between the quality of life and rates of personal violence holds only for some components of the quality of life index, in particular, education, health, demography, and welfare effort. These components are concerned with the psychological welfare of the individual (as compared to components such as geography, cultural diversity, and the defense effort).

Interestingly, the results differed for the smaller sample of industrialized nations. In these nations, the quality of life and its components were much less strongly associated with suicide rates, while still showing some relationship to homicide rates. Since the quality of life is much higher in the industrialized nations, it appears that, at high levels of quality, other variables determine suicide rates.

Table 14.3 The Association between Components of the Quality of Life and Rates of Personal Violence for 18 Nations in 1980

	Factor				
	I	*II*	*III*	*IV*	*V*
education	-0.10*	-0.01*	0.60*	0.28	0.37
health	0.06	0.06	-0.14	0.90*	-0.14
women's status	0.01	0.02	-0.06	-0.04	0.94*
defense effort	0.10	0.89*	-0.11	-0.12	-0.15
economy	-0.38	0.09	0.29	0.65*	0.28
demography	0.69*	0.45*	-0.04	0.39	-0.16
geography	0.94*	0.13	-0.02	-0.15	-0.14
political stability	-0.02	0.85*	-0.01	0.38	0.18
political participation	-0.07	-0.60*	0.68*	0.01	-0.20
cultural diversity	0.12	0.05	-0.92*	0.18	0.14
welfare effort	0.87*	-0.17	-0.22	-0.09	0.26
percent of variance	28%	21%	13%	12%	10%
correlation with					
suicide rate	0.14	0.37	-0.06	0.38	-0.18
homicide rate	-0.81#	-0.24	0.08	-0.11	0.20

* high loading (greater than 0.40)
# one-tailed significance less than 0.001

Table 14.4 Correlations between Changes in the Quality of Life
and Changes in Rates of Personal Violence from 1970 to 1980

	change in suicide rate	change in homicide rate	1980 suicide rate	1980 homicide rate
39 nations	0.03	0.07	0.07	0.06
18 nations	0.14	0.44*	0.07	0.60**

* one-tailed p < 0.05
** one-tailed p < 0.01

Changes in the quality of life from 1969 to 1979 were quite small. The correlation between the two sets of ratings in 1969 and 1979 was 0.92 for the 43 nations and 0.90 for the 18 industrialized nations. The mean quality of life for the 43 nations in 1979 was 145.2 and the mean increase since 1969 was only 2.2. (For the industrialized nations, the mean quality of life in 1979 was 173.6 and the mean increase since 1969 2.6.) It would be interesting to explore the relationship between changes in the quality of life and rates of personal violence over a time period in which greater changes took place in the quality of life.

DISCUSSION

The majority of these studies support the hypothesis derived from Henry and Short, with only one study finding no significant associations. The reasons for the discrepancy of the study using the 1981 data for SMSAs are not readily apparent. The discrepancy may be a result of the different era, the different type of geographical region chosen as the unit of study, and the different composition of the index of the quality of life.

For the association between the economic sub-indices and rates of personal violence, the results are not clear. The economic index correlated with rates of personal violence for the states of America, but not for nations of the world. Thus, the relationship between the particular social indicators used by those constructing the economic indices and rates of personal violence needs to be examined in much greater detail.

REFERENCES

Angoff, C., & Mencken, H. L. Worst American state. *American Mercury*, 1931, 24, 1-16, 175-188, 355-371.

Boyer, R., & Savageau, D. *Places rated almanac.* Chicago: Rand McNally, 1981.

Estes, R. J. *The social progress of nations.* New York: Praeger, 1984.

Henry, A. F., & Short, J. F. *Suicide and homicide.* New York: Free Press, 1954.

Lester, D. The association between the quality of life and suicide and homicide rates. *Journal of Social Psychology*, 1984, 124, 247-248.

Lester, D. The quality of life and suicide. *Journal of Social Psychology*, 1985a, 125, 279-280.

Lester, D. The quality of life in modern America and suicide and homicide rates. *Journal of Social Psychology*, 1985b, 125, 779-780.

Lester, D. Suicide, homicide, and the quality of life. *Suicide & Life-Threatening Behavior*, 1986, 16 389-392.

Lester, D. Quality of life and rates of suicide and homicide. *Perceptual & Motor Skills*, 1987, 64, 94.

Lester, D. The quality of life and suicide rates in American cities in 1930. *Psychological Reports*, 1989, 65, 1358.

Lester, D. Suicide, homicide and the quality of life in various countries. *Acta Psychiatrica Scandinavica*, 1990, 81, 332-334.

Porterfield, A., & Talbert, R. *Crime and well-being in your state and city.* Fort Worth: Texas Christian University Press, 1948.

APPENDIX A

Measurement Of The Quality Of Life

Education:
>
> school enrollment
>
> pupil-teacher ratio
>
> percent adult illiteracy
>
> percent GNP in education

Health:
>
> infant mortality rate
>
> population per physician
>
> male life expectancy at age 1

Women's Status:
>
> percent girls attending first level schools
>
> percent children in primary school who are female
>
> percent adult female illiteracy
>
> years since women's suffrage
>
> years since women suffrage equal to men

Defense Effort:
>
> percent GNP for defense spending

Economy:
>
> economic growth rate
>
> per capita income
>
> average annual rate of inflation
>
> per capita food production

Demography:
>
> total population
>
> crude birth rate
>
> crude death rate
>
> rate of population increase
>
> percent of population under 15 years

Geography:
>
> percent arable land mass

number major natural disaster impacts

lives lost in major natural disasters

Political Stability:

number of political protest demonstrations

number of political riots

number of political strikes

number of armed attacks

rate of death from domestic violence

Political Participation:

years since independence

years since most recent constitution

presence of functioning parliamentary system

presence of functioning political party system

degree of influence of military

number of popular elections held

Cultural Diversity:

largest percent sharing same mother tongue

largest percent sharing same basic religious belief

ethnic-linguistic fractionalization index

Welfare Effort:

years since first law for:

old age, invalidity, death

sickness and maternity

work injury

unemployment

family allowances

CHAPTER 15

THE RELATIVE ROLE OF SOCIAL AND ECONOMIC VARIABLES IN DETERMINING THE SUICIDE RATE

W e have conducted a number of studies in recent years on the relationship between the economy and suicide. Our research has examined both time-series trends and ecological variations (that is, variations over regions), both in the United States and in other nations. In this chapter we will review the findings of our research.

REGIONAL STUDIES IN THE UNITED STATES

A STUDY OF REAL INCOME

Yang (1989) used multiple regression analysis to investigate the relationship between economic conditions and suicide at the state level. She specified the following model for the determination of the suicide rate of a society.

$$S = f(Y, Y^2, DIV, MIG, FLFP, URB) + U$$

where
  S is the suicide rate
  Y is the real income per capita
  Y^2 is the square of the real income per capita
  DIV is the divorce rate

MIG is the amount of interstate migration
FLFP is the female labor force participation
URB is the percent of the population in urban areas
U is the stochastic disturbance term

Since the state is the unit of study and since the time dimension is not a variable, Yang argued that the impact of the business cycle on suicide at the state level should be the same for each state in terms of its direction, but not identical in terms of its extent, because each state is equipped with different facilities, private and public, accommodating the welfare and health problems arising in times of economic hardship. In general, the wealthier the state, the better its facilities will be. Likewise, in times of prosperity the wealthier states can better provide good services (private and public) to satisfy the public's needs (both material and cultural) than can less favored states.

The notion of the real income in each state was therefore important in determining the suicide rate. Yang chose to use the value of goods and services produced in the state to indicate the condition of the state's economy. The per capita state income was used as an indicator of the state's capacity for providing proper public and private goods and services for its inhabitants.[21] The square term of the per capita state income was added to explore the nonlinear relationship between the economic variables and the suicide rate.

The rest of Yang's model was based on Durkheim's theory of suicide. The concepts of social integration and regulation were operationalized through the social indicators of divorce, interstate migration, and urbanization. Divorce, according to Durkheim (1897), produces a lack of social control. The act of divorce breaks an institution which "regulates human wants, needs and sexual desires and relationships" (Vigderhous and Fishman, 1978, p. 246). Migration across state boundaries ruptures social relationships and decreases both social integration with and regulation by the original community for the migrants and exposes them to social isolation

---

[21] Brenner (1976) used the per capita income as one of the economic indicators in his aggregate longitudinal study. By using the per capita state income, we eliminate the possible impact of population size on the suicide rates.

in the new community. Urbanization may also create high levels of social isolation for city inhabitants. This social isolation, created either by inter-state migration or by urbanization, was conceived as "both a structural cause of and an individual motivation for suicide" (Taylor, 1982, p. 26).[22]

The impact of female participation in the labor force on the suicide rates was expected to work in two ways. On the one hand, women working creates a role conflict for them (Stack, 1978), which in turn decreases status integration (the degree to which statuses are associated in a social group). This, according to Gibbs and Martin (1964), leads to a higher sui-cide rate. On the other hand, participation in the labor force provides op-portunities for women to develop themselves more fully, which might help strengthen their social bonds and integration, leading to lower suicide rates. The net impact on the suicide rate depends, therefore, upon the rela-tive importance of these two effects. The labor force participation of women is positively associated with the divorce rate over states, though the causal connection remains unclear (e.g., Yeh and Lester, 1988).

Yang named her model a real income hypothesis of suicide, despite the presence of other social variables in the model, in order to emphasize the role of real income in the model and to indicate that real income is a better indicator of the state of the economy than other economic variables such as unemployment.

The unemployment rate reflects only the macroeconomic impact of the economy on the aggregate labor market. It overlooks the goods and serv-ices market and especially the assets market. Therefore, using the unem-ployment rate as an indicator of the state of the economy might introduce a severe bias. For example, an increased preference for leisure is often a typical by-product of a strong and prosperous economy. If the supply of labor remains the same, this will create a voluntary type of unemployment. Yet this type of unemployment definitely will not create misery or frustra-tion which might lead to an increased suicide rate.

---

[22] According to Taylor, Halbwachs (1930) attributed a high suicide rate in urban areas as compared to rural areas to a greater degree of social isolation in cities. For a detailed account of suicide and social isolation, see also Stengel (1964).

Yang put data from the 48 continental states of America in 1980 into a multiple regression analysis for the overall suicide rates, the male suicide rate, and the female suicide rate.

For the overall suicide rate, all the independent variables were significant and in the predicted direction except for urbanization and female participation in the labor force (see Table 15.1).

Table 15.1 Results of the Multiple Regression Analyses for the Suicide Rates of the Continental States of the United States in 1980 #

Dependent Variable	Independent Variables						
	GPPC	$GPPC^2$	IV	MIG	URB	FLFP	R
overall suicide rate	1.03* (2.08)	-1.01* (2.06)	0.38* (3.11)	0.57* (4.42)	-0.07 (0.77)	-0.12 (1.37)	.87
male suicide rate	1.33* (2.32)	-1.29* (2.31)	0.23 (1.73)	0.65* (4.32)	-0.20 (1.84)	-0.19 (1.89)	.82
female suicide rate	0.39 (0.76)	-0.43 (0.85)	0.54* (4.38)	0.33* (2.43)	0.21* (2.11)	0.01 (0.07)	.86

* significant at the 5% level or better

standardized regression coefficients are shown (with the t value in parentheses)

GPPC is the gross state product per capita and is a measure of the real income per capita.

The impact of a standardized unit of change in the per capita income on the suicide rate was negative and significant, implying that, though increases in income per capita have a negative impact on the suicide rate, that impact decreases as income continues to rise. The social integration/isolation effects on suicide as reflected by the divorce and interstate migration rates were positive.

The standardized regression coefficients allowed Yang to compare the relative importance of the independent variables. The order of magnitude of the impact of the variables indicated that the economic variables were more important in predicting the overall suicide rate of the states.

For the male suicide rate, only the income per capita, its square term and interstate migration had significant regression coefficients with plausible signs. The impact of a standardized unit of change in the per capita income on the suicide rate was negative and again greater than the impact of interstate migration. Urbanization and female participation in the labor force had a nonsignificant impact on the male suicide rate, though the contribution of these variables to this regression equation was greater than the contribution to the regression equation for the total suicide rate. Interestingly, the divorce rate did not exert a strong influence on the male suicide rate.

For the female suicide rate, the striking finding was that the economic variables played no significant role in the multiple regression though the signs of the regression coefficients were in the predicted direction. In contrast, the social variables of divorce, interstate migration, and urbanization emerged as the most powerful predictors of the female suicide rate. The sign of the coefficient for urbanization was positive, indicating that social isolation may play a role in determining the female suicide rate. The regression coefficient for female participation in the labor force was also positive, opposite in direction to its coefficient for the male suicide rate. Unfortunately, the levels of statistical significance for these coefficients were too low to permit reliable conclusions to be drawn.

Yang concluded that both economic variables (the gross state product per capita and its square) and sociological variables (the divorce rate and the rate of interstate migration) were statistically significant in predicting the overall suicide rates of the states. The results indicated that the economic variables were much more powerful predictors of the male suicide rates, with the rate of interstate migration playing a significant but lesser role. In contrast, the sociological variables were the more powerful predictors of the female suicide rates, with urbanization also playing a role, while the economic variables played no significant role. Further research is needed to explain the gender difference in these regression equations.

A Factor Analytic Approach

Lester has shown a preference for factor analysis over multiple regression analysis in his studies of regional suicide rates. Most ecological studies have used multiple regression analyses which Lester sees as arbitrarily selecting the most powerful correlates of the rates of personal violence. For example, let us assume that social indicator A correlates with a target variable with r = 0.81 and social indicator B correlates with r = 0.80. Although these two correlation coefficients are not significantly different, the multiple regression analysis may select social indicator A as the primary correlate, while social indicator B may not appear in the final multiple regression.

A factor analysis, on the other hand, groups all of the variables having strong intercorrelations together and permits an examination of how many clusters of social indicators exist and the extent to which they correlate with the target variables. Accordingly, Lester (1988) explored how a large set of socioeconomic indicators related to rates of personal violence (suicide and homicide) using a factor analysis of the social variables for the continental states of America in 1980.

The predictor variables were factor-analyzed using SPSSX (Anon, 1983) to perform a principal components extraction with a varimax rotation, and seven factors were identified. The factor scores for each factor were correlated with the suicide rates.

Suicide rates were significantly correlated with Factors III and IV. Factor III appeared to measure social instability with high loadings from the divorce rate, interstate migration and church attendance. Factor IV appears to measure an east-west, conservative dimension with high loadings from birth rate, longitude and the vote for Reagan as President.

Lester included several economic variables in his set of social variables: female participation in the labor force, married women working part-time and full-time, the unemployment rate (overall and for males), median family income, and the per capita income. None of these variables loaded on the factors that were associated with the state suicide rates.

Lester suggested that a useful way of conceptualizing the pattern of correlations between rates of personal violence and socioeconomic variables is to see the states of the United States as having different cultural patterns, some of which vary in an orderly manner across the country, from east to west and from north to south. To pick out one of the components of a pattern as supporting a particular hypothesis from theory and as the most important variable in predicting rates of personal violence obscures the fact that these components are related and are part of a broader cultural pattern.

Lester (1993a) confirmed that economic variables were, on the whole, unrelated to suicide rates over the states of America for males and females separately. Male and female participation in the labor force, percent in poverty, and male and female unemployment rates were unrelated to male suicide rates and to female suicide rates. The gross state product per capita was, however, positively related to both male and female suicide rates while the median income of women was related to the female suicide rate.

Lester then explored the association for blacks and whites. Unemployment rates and female participation in the labor force were unrelated to suicide rates in both whites and blacks. Median family income, however, was positively related to suicide rates in blacks.

Lester also explored the ability of socioeconomic variables to predict changes in the suicide rates of the states. Median personal income per capita and the unemployment rate were not associated with suicide rates and, furthermore, changes in the two economic variables were not associated with changes in the suicide rate from 1970 to 1980.

A Factor Analytic Exploration of Economic Variables and Suicide

To explore the relationship of economic variables with the suicide rates of the states of the United States in 1980, the economic variables in Lester's (1988) complete data set were subjected to a factor analysis using SPSSX, with a principal components extraction and a varimax rotation. The data used were obtained from the 1980 *Census Of The Population* or the *Statistical Abstract of the United States*, except where noted, and the variables included: the median family income, income per capita, personal income per capita, disposable income per capita, the total unemployment

Table 15.2 Factor Analysis of the Economic Variables of the States of America in 1980 and
Correlations with Rates of Personal Violence
(decimal points are omitted from the factor loadings)

rate	Factor				Correlations with total suicide
	I	*II*	*III*	*IV*	
median family income	87#	35	11	-20	-0.08
gross state product/cap	71#	01	-37	18	0.34
per capita income	95#	21	-05	-13	-0.01
personal income	95#	21	-05	-12	0.04
disposable income	94#	21	-06	-14	0.07
married women working:					
% full-time	-18	29	-19	88#	0.15
% part-time	21	62#	-14	-69#	-0.17
unemployment rate	-05	-23	96#	-07	-0.11
male unemployment	02	-20	91#	-18	-0.10
female unemployment	-15	-23	90#	13	-0.12
labor force participation:					
male	39	80#	-27	01	0.14
female	26	91#	-24	10	0.08
employment ratio	22	81#	-43#	07	0.16
% in poverty	-66#	-48#	01	40#	-0.02
percent of variance	49%	23%	9%	8%	
Correlations:					
suicide rate	0.10	-0.01	-0.14	0.25*	
homicide rate	0.09	- 0.50*	0.17	0.71*	
Suicide Rates:					
blacks	-0.06	0.10	0.04	-0.21	
whites	0.16	-0.13	-0.08	0.34*	
males	-0.01	-0.04	-0.13	0.17	
females	0.28	0.03	-0.10	0.30*	

Table 15.2 (Continued)

single males	-0.02	0.10	-0.15	-0.14
married males	-0.04	-0.05	-0.06	0.51*
divorced males	-0.23	-0.09	-0.11	0.02
widowed males	0.06	0.09	-0.25*	0.11
single females	0.23	0.14	-0.24	0.21
married females	0.16	0.13	-0.08	0.31*
divorced females	0.09	-0.12	0.01	0.07
widowed females	0.29*	-0.03	-0.27*	0.17
males:				
15-24	0.06	0.01	-0.22	-0.03
25-34	0.02	-0.13	0.04	0.05
35-44	-0.02	-0.06	0.09	0.18
45-54	-0.17	0.17	-0.06	0.34*
55-64	-0.03	-0.14	-0.26*	0.27*
65-74	-0.01	-0.10	-0.14	0.28*
75-84	-0.01	0.17	-0.11	0.16
85+	-0.13	0.21	0.22	0.11
females:				
15-24	0.05	0.20	-0.11	-0.12
25-34	0.24*	0.06	-0.07	0.43*
35-44	0.21	0.12	-0.09	0.13
45-54	0.07	0.07	-0.14	0.10
55-64	-0.10	0.04	0.12	0.03
65-74	0.19	-0.05	0.13	0.19
75+	0.06	-0.15	0.08	-0.13

high loading (> 0.40)
* significant at the 5% level or better

rate and the unemployment rates for men and women, the total labor force participation and the participation rates for men and women, the percent of married women working full-time and part-time, the percent of individuals in poverty, and the gross state product per capita (Renshaw, et al., 1988).

The simple Pearson correlations indicated that only the gross state product per capita was significantly associated with the suicide rates of the states (see Table 15.2). Disposable income per capita was associated with the female suicide rates of the states.

Four factors were identified from the factor analysis (see Table 15.2). Factor I had high loadings from the per capita income variables and the gross state product per capita and may be labeled an INCOME factor. Factor II had high loadings from participation of men and women in the labor force and the percent of married women working part-time, and may be labeled a LABOR FORCE PARTICIPATION factor. Factor III had high loadings from male and female unemployment, and may be labeled an UNEMPLOYMENT factor. Factor IV had high loadings from married women working part-time and may be labeled a FEMALE PART-TIME WORK factor.

The correlations between factors scores for these four factors and suicide rates are shown in Table 15.2. It can be seen that only scores on Factor IV (PART-TIME) correlated significantly with the overall suicide rate. In contrast, scores from both Factors II (LABOR FORCE PARTICIPATION) and IV (PART-TIME) correlated with homicide rates. Looking at the correlations of the economic factors with the suicide rates broken down by type of person, it can be seen that scores on Factor IV (PART TIME) were associated with the female suicide rate, the white suicide rate and the married persons suicide rate.

We must conclude that economic factors are only weakly associated with suicide rates at the state level in the United States, at least in 1980.

STUDIES OF COUNTIES IN THE UNITED STATES

Lester (1993a) examined the association between socioeconomic variables and suicide rates in the twenty-one counties of the state of New Jersey in 1980. Neither median family income nor the percentage below the poverty level was associated with the counties' suicide rates, paralleling the lack of an association at the state level. Lester (1992) found no association between male suicide and unemployment rates over twenty-three metropolitan areas of the United States in 1975.

REGIONAL STUDIES IN OTHER NATIONS

Lester has tried to replicate these studies with regional analyses of other nations. For example, Lester (1989a) looked at the association between male unemployment rates and female participation in the labor force over the twenty-two districts in Sri Lanka. Male unemployment was negatively related to the suicide rate in Sri Lanka (whereas there was no association over the states of the United States). Female participation in the labor force was unrelated to suicide rates in both nations.

Lester (1993a) examined the associations between socioeconomic variables and suicide rates over the counties in England. The average income was unrelated to suicide rates over English counties just as in the American states. The unemployment rates and suicide rates of Italian regions in 1986 were negatively associated, whereas there was no association over the states of America (Lester and Ausenda, 1993).

STUDIES OF NATIONS

Lester (1989b) explored the association of a number of socioeconomic variables with the suicide rates of eighteen modern nations. Using a factor analytic technique, he identified five clusters of variables (factors). The gross national product per capita loaded on the first factor, but this first factor was not associated with suicide rates. Female participation in the labor force and female economic equality loaded on the third factor, and this factor was positively associated with the suicide rates in 1970 but not with changes in the suicides rates in the following ten years.

Recently, Lester has compiled a data set consisting of the suicide rates of nations in the world in 1969 to 1971. For the present chapter, these suicide rates were correlated with a number of social and economic characteristics of the nations.

Suicide rates were available for fifty-seven nations, but data on social and economic variables were not always available for all of these nations. Real gross domestic products per capita were obtained for all of the nations from Summers and Heston (1984), but unemployment rates were available from the *Yearbook of Labor Statistics* published by the International Labor Office (Geneva) for only twenty-seven nations.

Table 15.3 Correlations between Social and Economic Variables
and Suicide Rates for Nations of the World in 1970

	Total Sample n=57	Western Europe n=15
population	0.02	-0.14
% 0-14	-0.74*	-0.68*
% 15-64	0.72*	0.47*
% 65+	0.70*	0.43
% urban population	0.34*	0.19
population density	0.06	-0.02
birth rate	-0.72*	-0.82*
death rate	-0.16	0.36
life expectancy	0.55	-0.06
fertility rate	-0.72*	-0.71*
RGDP	0.62*	0.78*
homicide rate	-0.42*	0.64*
divorce rate	0.63*	0.84*
marriage rate	0.43*	-0.23
area of country	0.03	-0.03
independence year	-0.26*	-0.23
emigration rate	0.16	-0.01
immigration rate	0.21	0.42
political rights	-0.14	-0.44*
civil rights	-0.13	-0.54*
unemployment	-0.37*	-0.34

The Pearson correlations between the suicide rates and the social and economic variables in the data set for the complete set of nations are shown in Table 15.3. Suicide rates correlated with the proportions of young, adult, and old people, the birth rate, life expectancies, fertility, real gross domestic product per capita, the homicide rate, the divorce rate, the marriage rate, the year of independence, and the unemployment rate. Table 15.3 also shows the correlations for the smaller subset of nations in Western Europe.

The correlation of suicide rates with the real gross domestic product per capita raises a problem in interpretation. It may well be that suicide is more common in nations that are wealthier. But it may also be that the more wealthier nations count suicides more accurately, whereas low suicide rates are reported in poorer nations because those nations do not count suicides completely.

In order to control for the association of the real gross domestic product on suicide rates, a partial correlation coefficient was calculated between the unemployment rate and the suicide rate controlling for the gross domestic product per capita. The partial correlation was -0.10 and not statistically significant. Thus, the wealth of the nations was positively associated with their suicide rates, but the unemployment rate was not.

Yang and Lester (1994c) found that the gross national product per capita and female labor force participation were associated with the suicide rates of men in fourteen Caribbean nations but not with the suicide rates of women.

TIME-SERIES STUDIES

Yang (1992 -- see also Lester, 1993b; Yang and Lester, 1994b) applied her real-income hypothesis of suicide to a study of suicide rates in the United States from 1940 to 1984. She examined the role played by the gross national product per capita (both without a lag and with a one year lag), the unemployment rate, female participation in the labor force, the divorce rate, the percentage of Roman Catholics, and the years of the Second World War in accounting for the suicide rate.

For the overall suicide rate, a multiple regression analysis indicated that the gross national product per capita (both without a lag and with a one year lag), the unemployment rate and female participation in the labor force all played a significant role in predicting the suicide rate. The effects of unemployment and the unlagged gross national product per capita were positive, while the effects of the lagged gross national product per capita and female participation in the labor force were positive.

Yang looked at the ability of these socioeconomic variables to predict the suicide rates of white males, white females, nonwhite males and nonwhite females separately. The lagged gross national product per capita had a negative influence for all four groups. Unemployment rates had a statistically significant influence only for white males. The unlagged gross national product per capita had a statistically significant influence only for white females and nonwhite females. Female participation in the labor force had a negative influence for females, a positive influence for nonwhite males and no influence for white males. Thus, it is clear that the relationship of these economic variables differs for the different groups.

Yang concluded that the beneficial impact of economic growth was present only for males. For females economic growth had a negative impact. With other variables held constant, both female participation in the labor force and unemployment rates had a rather modest impact on the suicide rate.

Yang (1990) also extended her analyses to different age groups. Using the same set of socioeconomic variables, she found that the association of unemployment with suicide rates was stronger in the younger groups (statistically significant only for those aged 15-24, 25-34 and 45-54). The association of female participation in the labor force with suicide rates was present for all age groups under 65 years of age, and the association of the unlagged gross national product per capita on those under 55 years of age. The association between the lagged gross national product per capita and suicide rates was found for all age groups.

The general conclusion appears to be that the effects of economic variables on suicide rate may be stronger in young adults than in older adults and those past retirement age, and these effects are negative. Times of economic prosperity are associated with higher suicide rate in younger adults.

Yang and Lester (1990) explored whether socioeconomic variables were more powerful in predicting the smoothed trend in the suicide rate (they used a five-year moving average) or the yearly fluctuations from this smoothed trend. They found that three of the four economic variables used (the growth in the gross national product, the unemployment rate and female participation in the labor force) all played a role in predicting the smoothed trend, the first two positively and the latter negatively. In contrast, while unemployment continued to play a positive role in predicting the fluctuations in the suicide rate from the smoothed trend, the growth in the gross national product now played a negative role and female participation in the labor force no role at all. Yang, et al. (1992b) extended this analysis by showing that fluctuations in the unemployment rate also predicted fluctuations in the suicide rate.

Yang and Lester (1922) showed that the association between unemployment and suicide was found in a time series analysis of monthly rates for the period 1957 to 1986 (the studies reported above used yearly rates), but not in a time series analysis of yearly rates, and Lester (1994b) showed that the association was found for each of the twelve months studied separately for this same time period.

Lester (1995b) factor-analyzed a large set of social variables for the United States for 1933-1985 and identified five independent factors. The factor scores were then placed in a multiple regression analysis to predict the suicide rate. Suicide rates of different demographic groups were most consistently predicted by the factors measuring military involvement (negatively) and business failures (positively).

Lester (1995c) found that the unemployment rate in New Mexico was significantly associated with the time series suicide rate of American Indians in that state, indicating that minority suicide rates may respond to the same socioeconomic conditions as the suicide rates of the dominant ethnic group.

THE UNITED STATES VERSUS OTHER NATIONS

Lester and Yang (1991) compared the results of time series analyses of data from the United States and Australia from 1946 to 1984. Unemployment rates were not associated with suicide rates in Australia, whereas the association with male suicide rates was positive in the United States. Participation in the labor force was positively associated with suicide rates in both men and women in Australia, but negatively with the male suicide rate in the United States. Thus, the results appear to depend upon the nation studied (as well perhaps as the time period chosen), and a single theory would have difficulty in accounting for all of the inconsistent results.

Yang, et al. (1992a) compared time-series data from the United States and Taiwan for the time period 1952 to 1984. For the United States, the gross national product per capita, unemployment, and divorce all had a positive impact in the multiple regression, female participation in the labor force had a negative impact, while the growth in the gross national product had no impact.

In contrast, in Taiwan, only divorce had a positive impact while female participation in the labor force continued to have a negative impact. Thus, one of the economic variables (female participation in the labor force) had a similar impact on suicide rates in the United States and Taiwan, while unemployment and the gross national product per capita had an impact only in the United States.

In a time series study comparing Canada and the United States from 1950-1985 (Leenaars, et al., 1993), social indicators (divorce, marriage and birth rates) were significant predictors of the suicide rate in both nations, while unemployment added no significant increment to the multiple regression. Unemployment was, however, positively associated with the suicide rate in both nations in a simple correlational analysis.

Lester and Natarajan (1995) found that the Indian suicide rate from 1969 to 1988 was predicted by female labor force participation (positively) and fertility (negatively), while in the United States these associations were reversed in direction. Lester (1995a) found that unemployment contributed to the prediction of the Quebec male suicide rate from 1951 to 1986 (along with birth, divorce and cirrhosis death rates), but not to the

Quebec female suicide rate. In New Zealand, from 1970 to 1989, unemployment contributed significantly to the prediction of white male youth suicide rates and to Maori male youth suicide rates, but not to female youth suicide rates, white or Maori (Lester, 1994b).

Yang and Lester (1994a, 1995; Lester and Yang, 1993) explored the association between unemployment and suicide in twelve nations for the period 1950-1985. Unemployment was significantly associated with suicide rates in only four nations. For percentage changes in these variables from year to year, only the United States, of the twelve nations studied, produced a significant association. Disaggregated data by age and gender were available for Canada, England and Wales and the United States, and the association between unemployment and suicide was significant in only 12 of the 42 regressions. For England and Wales there was some consistency, with three significant associations for men (for those aged 15-24, 35-44 and 45-54) and four negative associations for women (for those aged 15-24, 25-34, 35-44, 45-54).

DISCUSSION

We have reviewed in this chapter a large number of our studies (both regional and time-series) on the socioeconomic correlates of suicide rates. We have summarized the results in Table 15.4 to make it easy to examine the overall findings.

For the regional studies, it can be seen that only the gross domestic product per capita was associated with regional suicide rates, both over states and over nations. All of the other economic indicators, including participation in the labor force, personal income and unemployment rates, were not consistently associated with regional suicide rates.

Time-series studies, however, indicated that economic indicators played a major role in predicting suicide rates. The gross national product per capita was, in general, positively associated with suicide rates over time. The unemployment rate was positively associated with suicide rates while female participation in the labor force was negatively associated

Table 15.4 Summary of the Results of the Research Reviewed in this Chapter

	real gross state/domestic /national product	female labor force participation	unemployment	other economic variables
Regional Studies				
Yang (1989a): states				
total rate	+	ns		
male rate	+	ns		
female rate	ns	ns		
Lester (1990): states				
total rate	+	ns	ns	ns
male rate	+	ns	ns	ns
female rate	+	ns	ns	ns
Lester (1989a)				
Sri Lanka		ns		
Lester (1990)				
English counties:				
total rate				ns
Lester (1992):				
United States				
metropolitan areas			ns	
Lester (this book)				
nations	+		ns	
West Europe	+		ns	
Lester & Ausenda (1993)				
Italy			-	
United States			ns	

Table 15.4 (Continued)

Yang & Lester (1994c)			
Caribbean nations			
male rates	+	-	
female rates	ns	ns	
Time Series			
Yang (189b):			
United States 1940-1984			
total rate	+	-	+
white male	ns	ns	+
white female	+	-	ns
nonwhite male	ns	+	ns
nonwhite female	+	-	ns
15-24 year	+	-	+
25-34 year	+	-	+
35-44 year	+	-	ns
45-54 year	+	-	+
55-64 year	ns	-	ns
65+ years .	ns	ns	ns
Yang & Lester (1990)			
United States 1940-1984			
total rate	+	-	+
smoothed rate	ns	-	+
fluctuations	ns	ns	+
Yang, et al. (1992b)			
United States 1940-1984			
smoothed variables	+	-	+
fluctuations	ns	-	+
Yang & Lester (1992)			
United States, 1957-1986			
monthly			+
yearly			ns

Table 15.4 (Continued)

Lester (1994b) *United States, 1957-1988* January, February, etc.			+ (for ten months)[*] - for two months	
Lester (1995b) *United States, 1933-1985* white males				-
nonwhite males				-
white females				ns
nonwhite females				ns
15-24, 25-34, 35-44				ns
45-54, 55-64, 65+				-
Lester (1993b): *1967-1986* white males			ns	ns
white females			ns	ns
nonwhite males			ns	ns
nonwhite females			ns	ns
Lester (1995c): *New Mexico* American Indians, 1958-1986			+	
Lester & Yang (1990) *United States 1946-1984* total rate		-	ns	
male rate		-	+	
female rate		ns	ns	
Australia 1946-1984 total rate		+	ns	
male rate		+	ns	
female rate		+	ns	

[*] Two were statistically significant

Table 15.4 (Continued)

Yang, et al. (1992a)			
United States 1952-1984			
total rate	+	-	+
Taiwan 1952-1984			
total rate	ns	-	ns
Lester (1994a)			
New Zealand 1970-1989			
Maori male youth			+
other male youth			+
Maori female youth			ns
other female youth			ns
Leenaars, et al. (1993):			
1950-1985			
Canada			ns
United States			ns
Lester & Yang (1993):			
1950-1985			
Denmark			ns
Finland			ns
Netherlands			+
Norway			ns
Yang & Lester (1994a):			
1950-1985			
Taiwan			+/+
United States			+/+
Denmark			+/ns
Japan			+/ns
Netherlands			+/ns
Norway			+/ns
Austria			ns
Belgium			ns
Canada			ns
England/Wales			ns
Sweden			ns

Table 15.4 (Continued)

West Germany		ns
Canada: age by gender		ns
United States:		ns
age by gender		
England/Wales:		
men: by age		+
women: by age		-
Yang & Lester (1995):		
1950-1985 (% changes0		
United States		+
11 other nations		ns
Lester & Natarajan		
(1995)		
India, 1969-1988	+	
United States:	-	
1969-1988		
Lester (1995a)		
Quebec, 19561-1986		
men		+
women		ns

with suicide rates.

However, it should be noted that these relationships were not consistently found in nations other than the United States, and so the world-wide generality of these conclusions must be explored further.

The research indicates, therefore, considerable discrepancies between the results of regional and of time-series studies. It would appear that no simple theory will be able to account for the results of both types of studies (Lester, 1993c).

REFERENCES

Anon. *SPSSX user's guide.* New York: McGraw-Hill, 1983.

Durkheim, E. *Le suicide.* Paris: Alcan, 1897.

Gibbs, J. D., & Martin, W. T. *Status integration and suicide.* Eugene: University of Oregon, 1964.

Halbwachs, M. *Les causes du suicide.* Paris: Felix Alcan, 1930.

Leenaars, A. A., Yang, B., & Lester, D. The effect of domestic and economic stress on suicide rates in Canada and the United States. *Journal of Clinical Psychology,* 1993, 49, 918-921.

Lester, D. A regional analysis of suicide and homicide rates in the USA. *Social Psychiatry & Psychiatric Epidemiology,* 1988, 23, 202-205.

Lester, D. A regional analysis of suicide: the USA vs Sri Lanka. *Social Psychiatry,* 1989a, 24, 143-145.

Lester, D. National suicide and homicide rates. *Social Science & Medicine,* 1989b, 29, 1249-1252.

Lester, D. Unemployment, suicide and homicide in metropolitan areas. *Psychological Reports,* 1992, 71, 558.

Lester, D. *Patterns of suicide and homicide in America.* Commack, NY: Nova Science, 1993a.

Lester, D., Economic status of African-Americans and suicide rates. *Perceptual & Motor Skills,* 1993b, 77, 1150.

Lester, D. Time-series versus regional correlates of rates of personal violence. *Death Studies,* 1993c, 17, 529-534.

Lester, D. Maori and nonMaori youth suicide. *New Zealand Medical Journal,* 1994a, 107, 161.

Lester, D. Suicide and unemployment. *Psychological Reports,* 1994b, 75, 602.

Lester, D. Suicide in Quebec, *Psychological Reports,* 1995a, 76, 122.

Lester, D. Combining opposing methodologies in studies of suicide and homicide. *Quality & Quantity,* 1995b, 29, 67-72.

Lester, D. American Indian suicide rates and the economy. *Psychological Reports,* 1995c, 77, 994.

Lester, D., & Ausenda, G. The regional variation of suicide in Italy and the USA. *Italian Journal of Suicidology*, 1993, 3, 97-99.

Lester, D., & Natarajan, M. Predicting the time series suicide and murder rates in India. *Perceptual & Motor Skills*, 1995, 80, 570.

Lester, D., & Yang, B. The relationship between divorce, unemployment and female participation in the labor force and suicide rates in Australia and America. *Australian & New Zealand Journal of Psychiatry*, 1991, 25, 519-523.

Lester, D., & Yang, B. Anticipating the impact of the high unemployment rate in Eastern Europe. *Current Politics & Economics of Europe*, 1993, 3(1), 33-35.

Renshaw, V., Trott, E. A., & Friedenberg, H. L. Gross state product by industry. *Survey of Current Business*, 1988, May, 30-46.

Stack, S. Suicide. *Social Forces*, 1978, 57, 644-653.

Summers, R., & Heston, A. Improved international comparisons of real product and its composition. *Review of Income & Wealth*, 1984, 30, 207-262.

Taylor, S. *Durkheim and the study of suicide.* New York: St. Martin's, 1982.

Vigderhous, G., & Fishman, G. The impact of unemployment and family integration on changing suicide rates in the USA, 1920-1969. *Social Psychiatry*, 1978, 13, 239-248.

Yang, B. A real income hypothesis of suicide: a cross-sectional study of the United States. Eastern Economic Association, Baltimore, March 1989.

Yang, B. The impact of the economy on suicide in different social and demographic groups. Eastern Economic Association, Cincinnati, 1990.

Yang, B. The economy and suicide. *American Journal of Economics & Sociology*, 1992, 51, 87-99.

Yang, B., & Lester, D. Time-series analyses of the American suicide rate. *Social Psychiatry & Psychiatric Epidemiology*, 1990, 25, 274-275.

Yang, B., & Lester, D. Suicide, homicide and unemployment. *Psychological Reports*, 1992, 71, 844-846.

Yang, B., & Lester, D. The social impact of unemployment. *Applied Economics Letters*, 1994a, 1, 223-226.

Yang, B., & Lester, D. Crime and unemployment. *Journal of Socio-Economics*, 1994b, 23, 215-222.

Yang, B., & Lester, D. Economic and social correlates of suicide in Caribbean nations. *Psychological Reports*, 1994c, 75, 351-352.

Yang, B., & Lester, D. Suicide, homicide and unemployment. *Applied Economics Letters*, 1995, 2, 278-279.

Yang, B., Lester, D., & Yang, C. H. An economic theory of suicide revisited: a comparison of the USA and Taiwan. *Social Science & Medicine*, 1992a, 34, 333-334.

Yang, B., Stack, S., & Lester, D. Suicide and unemployment. *Journal of Socio-Economics*, 1992, 21, 39-41.

Yeh, B. Y., & Lester, D. Statewide divorce rates and wives' participation in the labor market. *Journal of Divorce*, 1988, 11, 107-114.

PART 5:

CONCLUSIONS

CHAPTER 16

CONCLUSIONS

We have tried in this volume to document the importance of the economy in the determination of suicidal behavior and the usefulness of economic models in accounting for suicidal behavior. In this final chapter, we will briefly summarize our conclusions and point to issues which promise to be most fruitful for future research.

THE ECONOMIC COST OF SUICIDE

In Chapter 2, we documented that suicide and its lesser manifestations, such as depression, incur great costs for the society, both in the loss of life when people kill themselves and in the care that must be taken of those who are suicidal but who do not die.

It should be noted that psychologists and psychiatrists have long speculated that the suicidal impulse does not manifest itself only in suicide (for example, Menninger, 1938; Farberow, 1980). Rather, it may motivate many all kinds of self-destructive behaviors, including the "chronic suicide" of the alcohol and drug abuser, the accident proneness of some individuals, the failure of patients to take their life-sustaining medications, and eating disorders (both those who are obese and those who are anorexic).

If we include these lesser manifestations of the suicidal impulse, then the economic costs of self-destructive impulses are enormous.

THE BUSINESS CYCLE AND SUICIDE

We described in Part 2 the three major theories which relate the business cycle to suicide: Durkheim's theory that suicide is more common in times of expansion and contraction, Ginsberg's theory that suicide is more common in times of expansion, and Henry and Short's theory that suicide is more common in times of contraction. We indicated in Chapter 6 that the research to test the validity of these alternative theories has not yet advanced very far. Rather, investigators have sought to conduct simple correlational studies of the relationship between economic variables and suicide rates that do not test these theories precisely. Much work needs to be done to find out which of the theories has validity and under what circumstances.

ECONOMIC MODELS OF SUICIDE

In Part 3, we tried to show how standard economic theories could be applied to the seemingly irrational behavior of suicide. We showed that suicide could be fitted into a supply-and-demand model, a utility model, a cognitive filtering model of choice, and a labor-market perspective. Economists have rarely applied their theories to an analysis of suicidal behavior, and we hope that the efforts reported here will stimulate other economists to further work in this area.

THE ECONOMY AND SUICIDE

In Part 4, we reviewed the considerable body of work which has been published by economists, psychologists, and sociologists on the relationship between economic variables and suicide. It is very clear from this review that a connection has been thoroughly established, especially for the economic variable of unemployment.

One feature of the research which promises to intrigue future researchers is the discrepancies between regional studies and time-series studies. For example, the relationship between unemployment and suicide is clearer for time-series studies than for regional studies. A single theory, therefore, is unlikely to be able to explain both time-series and regional phenomenon, though some scholars disagree (Simon, 1968).

Another feature of this research which promises to be productive in the future is why the findings often do not generalize to other nations, for example, Lester and Yang's (1991) finding that unemployment is associated with the American suicide rate over time but not with the Australian suicide rate. As more of the research is repeated in other nations, we will be able to find which research findings and which theories are nation-specific and which have greater generality.

Thus, in conclusion, we have shown that study of economic aspects of suicide is a burgeoning and important area of research, and we hope our volume stimulates others to pursue these important issues.

REFERENCES

Farberow, N. L. *The many faces of suicide.* New York: McGraw-Hill, 1980.

Lester, D., & Yang, B. The relationship between divorce, unemployment and female participation in the labor force and suicide rates in Australia and America. *Australian & New Zealand Journal of Psychiatry*, 1991, 25, 519-523.

Menninger, K. *Man against himself.* New York: Harcourt Brace, 1938.

Simon, J. L. The effect of income on the suicide rate. *American Journal of Sociology*, 1968, 74, 302-303.

Name Index

A

Abe, K., 125, 130
Ahlburg, D. A., 104, 109, 114, 116, 126, 129, 130
Akerlof, G., 73, 79
Allander, E., 116
Alston, M. H., 113, 115, 116
Angoff, C., 133, 141
Araki, S., 126, 130
Aristidou, M., 117
Arnetz, B. B., 110, 116
Ausenda, G., 155, 162, 168

B

Babigan, H. M., 100, 118
Baker, L., 117
Barnes, C., 56
Baruch, G. K., 116
Bauer, R., 117
Beaumont, J. J., 111, 116
Becker, G. S., 68, 79, 91, 93, 95, 96
Bedeian, A., 116
Berman, A. L., 121, 125
Berney, B. W., 116
Birmingham, P., 109, 116
Black, R., 79
Blair, A., 110, 116
Blazer, D., 10
Bluestone, B., 103, 117
Boor, M., 105, 117
Borg, S. E., 102, 117
Borges, S., 122
Bourque, L., 119
Boyd, J. H., 53, 56
Boyer, R., 135, 141
Brandt, R. B., 87, 88
Breault, K. D., 103, 114, 117, 126, 128, 130

Brenner, M. H., 104, 117, 127, 128, 130, 146
Brinkerhoff, M., 109, 114, 119, 128, 130
Brooke, E. M., 121

C

Camerer, C., 77, 79
Carlson, G. A., 112, 117
Catalano, R. A., 99, 104, 107, 117, 118
Charlton, J. R., 117
Chisholm, L., 117
Christoffersen, K., 118
Clarke, R. V., 53, 54, 56, 57, 111, 117
Clayden, D., 103, 121
Cormier, H. J., 105, 117
Craig, A. G., 117
Crombie, I. K., 103, 105, 117
Crouch, R., 60, 61, 65
Crowle, J., 118
Cumming, E., 100, 113, 115, 117

D

Danigelis, N., 126, 131
Davis, L. K., 110, 117
Davis, R., 114, 118
De Hart, C., 110, 118
Depue, R. H., 118
Dickens, W. T., 79
Diggory, J. D., 118
Dollard, J., 23, 25, 28
Doob, L., 28
Dooley, D., 99, 107, 117, 118
Duffy, J. C., 107, 121

SUBJECT INDEX